JACQUES MARITAIN

Bronze bust of Jacques Maritain by sculptor Alex Giampietro, Washington, D.C.

Jude P. Dougherty

JACQUES MARITAIN

An Intellectual Profile

* * *

The Catholic University of America Press
Washington, D.C.

The paper used in this publication meets the minimum
requirements of American National Standards for Information
Science—Permanence of Paper for Printed Library materials,
ANSI Z39.48-1984.

∞

Library of Congress Cataloging-in-Publication Data

Dougherty, Jude P., 1930–
    Jacques Maritain : an intellectual profile /
Jude P. Dougherty.
        p.   cm.
Includes bibliographical references and index.
    ISBN 0-8132-1329-0 (pbk. : alk. paper)
    1. Maritain, Jacques, 1882–1973.   I. Title.
    B2430.M34 D68 2003
    194—dc21
                            2002151510

CONTENTS

JACQUES MARITAIN

INTRODUCTION

Maritain's long and varied career is a chronicle of his time as well as a personal journey. From the feet of Leon Bloy to the French Ambassadorship to the Holy See, his intellectual compass provided an undeviating course. The youthful French intellectual discovering and embracing the Catholic Faith and then his subsequent discovery of St. Thomas Aquinas is almost a story in itself. His newfound intellectual confidence led him to critique the philosophy of his mentor, Henri Bergson. The eminent Bergson had reason to be chagrined at the apostasy of one of his most promising students. Maturation brought Maritain to a renewed appreciation of Bergson as he simultaneously delved deeper into the philosophy of Aquinas. The peasant of the Garonne, as he was later to call himself, early on delivered a scathing attack on three reformers, Luther, Descartes, and Rousseau. Though he subsequently moderated his tone, his critical intelligence never failed him.

Critiques aside, Maritain began a lifelong study of the philosophy of Aquinas and its implication for modern thought. He was not a textual exegete, but a speculative philosopher who thought *ad mentem divi Thomae*. Maritain insisted that he was not a neo-Thomist but a Thomist. The *Distinguer pour unir; ou les degrés du savoir* (1932), *Court traité de l'existence et de l'existant* have been read by generations of students worldwide. His *Art et scolastique* (1920) has become a Christian classic, and decades later it was followed by *Creative Intuition in Art and Poetry* (1953).

Two of the early works were translated from French into Italian by Giovanni Battista Montini, the future Paul VI, then a seminary professor. The gentle and reserved Maritain was all tooth and claw in intellectual debate. In disagreement he could be harsh and caustic. Etienne Gilson, by contrast, usually challenged ideas in their context. The historian of philosophy could not disengage ideas from their holder or the intellectual milieu from which they arose. Maritain would attack adverse positions in their pure and abstract form, often with pain to the subject of his criticism. From a Thomistic position he challenged the materialisms, positivisms and determinisms of his day. This led to an invitation of the French bishops to do a series of textbooks in philosophy for use in the seminaries. Of a projected seven volumes, he completed only two, *An Introduction to Logic* and *An Introduction to Philosophy*, although subsequent writing covered most of the topics initially planned for coverage. His wife Raïssa was not a philosopher, but clearly she was an intellectual peer. Their omnivorous interest in the arts and sciences attracted a wide circle of friends, philosophers, theologians, painters, and poets, who would gather at the Maritain home in Meudon on Sunday afternoons, among them Garrigou-Lagrange, Jean Cocteau, Etienne Gilson, Ernst Psichari, Nicholas Berdyaev, Emmanuel Mounier, François Mauriac, Marc Chagall, and Georges Rouault. In 1914 when Maritain joined the faculty of the Institut Catholique de Paris, the Thomistic revival was well underway, and Maritain was making a major contribution. His writing led him to lecture tours in North and South America. Translated into Spanish and Portugese, his work was particularly influential in Brazil and Argentina, an influence that today remains unabated in Catholic circles.

Although Maritain's interest in social and political issues is evident in *Humanisme intégral* (1936), it is generally acknowledged that his best work in social and political philosophy was accomplished in his North American years. The Walgreen lectures, delivered at the University of Chicago in 1949, must be considered of perennial value and a major contribution to Catholic political thought. *Christianity and Democracy* and *Education at the Crossroads* were written while he was in exile from his native France. When France fell in 1940, Maritain was on a lecture tour in the United States, where he remained until the close of the war. The lucidity of his work gained for him a following outside of professional circles. Called to address some of the major policy issues of the day, he participated in the drafting of the United Nations Universal Declaration of Human Rights at San Francisco in 1945. He weekly provided occupied France with uplifting radio broadcasts.

Robert M. Hutchins as chancellor of the University of Chicago tried twice to appoint him to its faculty of philosophy. Each time his nomination was blocked at the departmental level. Denied an appointment at Chicago, he was eventually appointed at Princeton University, a position he accepted when he was 65 years of age and which he held from 1948 to 1952.

Devastated by the death of Raïssa, he spent his final years with the Little Brothers of Jesus, whose house was in the garden of the Dominican Convent on the banks of the Garonne in Toulouse.

The author of more than fifty books, the entry for Maritain in the French "Who's Who" lists him as a philosopher and man of letters. He was honored as both. In addition to many academic honors, Maritain was named a Commander of the Legion of Honor and a Knight Commander of the Order of St. Gregory the Great. He was also given the Medal of the French Resistance and the Grand Cross of the Order of Pius IX. As a writer he received the *Grand Prix* of Literature from the French Academy in 1961 and the French National Grand Prize for letters in 1963.

While Maritain is venerated by many, he has not been without detractors, which is to be expected among those who espouse a pragmatic naturalism or antimetaphysical, purely empirical approach to philosophy. In Catholic academic circles, his *Paysan de la Garonne* (1966) scandalized the left because Maritain seemingly vacated many of the liberal policies he formerly embraced. His last two works, *Approches sans entraves* (1973) and *De l'Église du Christ* (1973), were given scant notice by the Catholic press in North America. In his later works, Maritain voiced concern over some of the practices that had been introduced into his beloved Catholic Church in the post-Vatican II years, practices which found little support in the Council documents themselves but were inspired by what some progressive theologians called the "spirit of Vatican II." Once again he proved to be prescient. His concerns are almost universally recognized, and we now find Vatican officials trying to restore a respect for some of the practices hastily abandoned.

It is impossible to assess Maritain's lasting contribution to Catholic thought. Paul VI called Maritain his teacher and cited him in *Popularum Progressio* (1967). Yves Simon, a student when Maritain taught at the Institut Catholique, acknowledged his mentor's influence as he developed his political philosophy. So too did John Courtney Murray when speaking of the role of religion in society and the relation of the church to the state. It is evident that Etienne Gilson was influenced by Maritain's insistence on the existential character of Thomistic metaphysics. Both stressed the importance of judgment as relevatory of *esse* (the act of *being*), and of Maritain's point to the intuitive and affective character of the juridicative act. Their common concern was to avoid what was thought to be a static essentialism in which even the act of being was conceptually represented as a thing. Many of their common disciples in North America helped develop a metaphysics of *esse*, including Joseph Owens, Gerard Smith, George Klubertanz, and

Anton Pegis. In France, E. Mounier oscillated from discipleship to flirtation with the fascists and eventually to brief cooperation with the French Communist Party. Maritain's influence on the Personalist movement was pronounced. Jean-Paul Sartre complained to Denis de Rougemont, "You Personalists have won . . . everybody in France calls himself a Personalist."

The interest in Maritain's work continues unabated throughout the West. One finds institutes and conferences built around Maritain's legacy in Europe and North and South America. Eugeen de Jonge, the late editor of *Politica* (Belgium), and Bishop Nicholas Derisi, long-time editor of the quarterly *Sapientia* (Argentina), provided forums for discussions of his social and political philosophy.

Foremost among contemporary disciples of Maritain is Ralph McInerny, director of the Jacques Maritain Center at the University of Notre Dame. With his encouragement the University of Notre Dame Press has undertaken the publication of the English-language translations of Maritain's *oeuvre* in a uniform edition. McInerny is not only instrumental in making available the written work of Maritain, but through the Maritain Center has provided students and seasoned scholars with the opportunity to study Maritain's works as well as those of St. Thomas Aquinas. The portrait which appears as a frontispiece to this volume is a photograph of a bust commissioned by McInerny and executed by Alex Giampietro of Washington, D.C. Declared by viewers to be of museum quality, a copy of the bust was presented to Pope John Paul II with the hope that it might grace a portal within the Vatican where Maritain served for three years as ambassador.

On a personal note, my first encounter with Maritain occurred when as a college student in the junior seminar of the School of Philosophy at The Catholic University of America I was obliged to read his *Introduction to Philosophy*. Later I was privileged to attend his A. W. Mellon Lectures at the National Gallery of Art in Washington, D.C., lectures that became *Creative Intuition in Art and Poetry*. As a graduate student the first paper I read to the graduate student colloquium was on Maritain's philosophy of science. The first paper I gave to a college faculty was on Maritain's *Man and the State*. Years later Thomas Merton shared with me some of his personal correspondence with Maritain whose handwriting at that time indicated clearly that he was in decline.

The essays presented in this volume explore only a fraction of Maritain's wide-ranging intellect. They offer an appreciation of the perennial value of his work in metaphysics, the philosophy of art, and social and political philosophy. They were delivered as lectures in places as distant as Venice, Pamplona, and Buenos Aires.

As a model of the philosopher working within the Catholic faith and drawing upon antiquity and the Middle Ages, principally Aquinas, to address contemporary issues, Maritain is likely to be unsurpassed. In the twentieth century he preeminently represented the *philosophia perennis* and has thereby earned the accolade of "doctor of the Church."

MARITAIN ON CHURCH AND STATE

I

It is hazardous to talk about the relation of church and state in the abstract, as if there were an ideal relationship to be achieved and against which all others are to be measured. The *modus vivendi* which prevailed in Greece and Rome during the classical period could not have been culturally possible in China of the same era. Later the religious paternalism of the Greek city-state or of the Roman *polis* became impossible from the standpoint of Christianity. The doctrine of two swords was forged early, and since Ambrose it has remained the standard in the West.[1] Even Ambrose's relation as Bishop of Milan to the Emperor Theodosius I was quite different from that which was to prevail a hundred years later between Pope Gelasius and Anastasius, the Emperor of Constantinople, and both those relationships were far different from that which was to obtain between Abbot Suger of Saint Denis and Louis VI, who copiously endowed the Abbey Church, and Louis, VII, who made Suger regent of France as he joined a crusade to restore the Holy Land to Christendom.[2] The medieval problem is not the modern prob-

1. See Claudio Morino, *Church and State in the Teaching of St. Ambrose*, trans. M. Joseph Costelloe (Washington, D.C.: The Catholic University of America Press, 1969).
2. See Otto von Simson, "Suger of St. Denis," *The Gothic Cathedral* (New York: Pantheon, 1962), 61–90.

lem, just as the church-state relationship in Spain is not that of Poland, and that in England is not that of the United States. Mindful of context, still we need not despair of enunciating principle.

Maritain's treatment of church-state problems, although colored by twenty centuries of history, nevertheless flows principally from an analysis of certain accepted basic principles in human nature and in social structures. It was never Maritain's intention, nor is it ours, to review the vast literature on church and state; still, there are valuable lessons to be learned from the past. History is illuminating as it displays men of differing times and different cultures grappling with what seems to be a universal problem of governance.

The philosopher's approach to the problem, if not in all respects identical with that of the perspective of the state, is nevertheless one which views religion from a secular perspective. Thus we may ask, from the point of view of the state, does it make a difference whether men believe in and worship God? Does society have a stake in the presence or absence of religion? Should governments encourage, remain indifferent to, or actively oppose religion?

In the classical period of Western culture, the state's interest in religion was taken for granted. The age of Greek political experience admits of no distinction between church and state. The Greek *polis* can only be described as both a state and a church. Both Plato and Aristotle assumed the *polis* or *res publica* to be the highest expression of the common good, that is, the embodiment of a moral value.[3] The whole destiny of man was involved in the state. The Roman world because of empire was more complex than the Greek, forcing the Romans to focus on implementing structure where the Greek was principally concerned with ends. Cicero of-

---

3. Cf. Alexander P. d'Entrèves, *The Notion of the State* (Oxford: Clarendon Press, 1967), chap. 3.

fers the most detailed treatment in his treatise, *De legibus,* where he provides a description of priestly function within the ideal society.[4] Cicero explores, first, the means by which the state should endeavor to win the favor of the gods and, second, the ways by which the state under divine favor should live and function. To achieve the first end, the state acts through religious ceremony and priestly order; to achieve the second, it acts through magistrates and the groupings of the chief men and people.

Cicero goes on to describe the manner in which the gods should be approached, distinguishing first a hierarchy among the gods and, then, between urban and rural ceremonial practices. Recognizing the importance of religion in the countryside, he decrees days of relaxation, falling at such seasons of the year as naturally coincide with the end of the farmer's labor. In the cities, on the other hand, the gods are to be worshiped in temples, where statues bring the gods vividly before the eyes and thoughts of men. The chief and preeminent power in the commonwealth is that associated with the authority of the augurs. Their pronouncements are law to the commanders in the field and to the magistrates in the city. Declaring war, concluding peace, or striking a treaty is done with sanction of religion. It was a common acknowledgment among the Romans that political power, considered abstractly, flowed from the gods. Human agents could properly exert political authority only when that authority was divinely sanctioned.[5]

Against this cultural backdrop it is no mystery that Ambrose could force the Emperor Theodosius to repent publicly in the basilica of Milan of his sin against Salonica.[6] This occurred in

---

4. *De legibus,* Loeb Classical Library (Cambridge: Harvard University Press, 1966), Bk. II, chap. 8ff.

5. Ibid., chap. 9.

6. For accounts of Ambrose's relationship to Theodosius, see Angelo Paredi, *St. Ambrose: His Life and Times* (Notre Dame: University of Notre Dame Press, 1964); John

380, only a few decades after Christianity had emerged from the catacombs. The way had been prepared. The distinction between things temporal and things spiritual had been clearly made in Roman times and a hierarchy established.

Nearer home, and the immediate backdrop to Maritain's discussions, is the solution to the problem of church and state as worked out by the Founding Fathers of the United States. The spokesmen for the colonists took for granted the good effects of religion. The problem at hand was that of the adjudication of conflict among a multiplicity of sects. George Mason's draft of the Virginia Bill of Rights provided that men should enjoy "the fullest toleration in the exercises of religion."[7] His colleague, James Madison, thought stronger language was needed since toleration could be taken to mean only a limited form of religious liberty, i.e., the toleration of dissenters in a state where there was an established church. Madison drafted a substitute declaring that "all men are equally entitled to the full and free exercise of religion," and, therefore, "that no man or class of men ought, on account of religion, to be invested with any peculiar emoluments or privileges."[8] Madison was writing in a state that did in fact have an established church, and it was not his intent to disestablish the Anglican Church in Virginia. Thus Virginia was permitted to retain her established church, and dissenters were guaranteed tolerance. Out of the Virginia debate came the adoption of the First Amendment to the United States Constitution with its declaration that Congress shall make "no law respecting an establishment of religion or prohibiting the free exercise thereof."

Matthews, *Western Aristocracies and the Imperial Court* (Oxford: Clarendon Press, 1975); and N. Q. King, *The Emperor Theodosius and the Establishment* (Philadelphia: Westminster Press, 1960).

7. *The Papers of George Mason 1725–1791*, ed. Robert A. Rutland (Chapel Hill: University of North Carolina Press, 1970), 1:278.

8. *The Papers of James Madison*, ed. William T. Hutchinson and William M. E. Rachals (Chicago: University of Chicago Press, 1962), 1:174.

It is only within the past forty years that the United States Supreme Court has produced a significant gloss on the Constitution's First Amendment.[9] In those forty years the neutrality doctrine which governed legislation and the courts in the early days of the Republic came to be construed not simply as neutrality between sects but a neutrality between religion and irreligion. Legislation affecting religion, the court came to hold, must have a secular purpose and a primary effect that neither advances nor inhibits religion. While Justice William Douglas in the Zorach decision (1952) may have reflected the sentiment of the court when he wrote, "We are a religious people whose institutions presuppose a Supreme Being," before his death he was to emerge as a spokesman for an entirely different doctrine, namely, that of benevolent neutrality which affirms that the state does not have a stake in the success of religion. Such a turn might have surprised Jefferson who, while he spoke of "a wall of separation," never wanted to divorce religion from public life. Like Hobbes and Locke he believed in the social utility of religion. Commonly held religious beliefs are necessary to the smooth functioning of the body politic. Religious people make the best citizens. But it is not necessary to have an established church to get the benefits of religion in the civic arena. Small churches, as voluntary societies, can accomplish quite automatically all that is claimed for an established church and without the cumbersome operations of state power behind them.

The Enlightenment rationalization of which Jefferson was a representative emphasized a belief in the sufficiency of human reason applied to all aspects of life. Belief in God was part of the system, but it was a God who had created the universe and set it to run according to immutable laws, both physical and moral. Man's part is to discover these laws and to conduct his life accordingly.

9. See A. E. Dick Howard, "Up Against the Wall: The Uneasy Separation of Church and State," *Church, State, and Politics*, ed. Jaye B. Hensel (Washington, D.C.: The Roscoe Pound American Trial Lawyers Foundation, 1982), 5–39.

The essence of religion is morality, that is, living according to the eternal principles of right and wrong, principles which are discernible by the free operation of human reason. Jefferson held that this pure moral code of religion found its perfection of expression in the teachings of Jesus, teachings which were, however, unfortunately entangled in a web of irrelevant doctrine. Jefferson's attempt to free this teaching from its dogmatic shackles is well known. He created his own version of the New Testament, selecting those sayings of Jesus which he considered indubitably authentic.

II

Since the Enlightenment the West has witnessed the emergence of a set of views which help explain contemporary attitudes toward religion. Voltaire urged the eradication of Christianity from the world of higher culture, but he was willing to have it remain in the stables and in the scullery.[10] Mill repudiated Christianity, but not the religion of humanity which he thought to be, from the point of view of the state, a useful thing.[11] Comte, more benevolent in his attitude to Christian practice than either Voltaire or Mill, and in spite of denial of all metaphysical validity to religious belief, was willing to accept as a civic good the moral and ritual traditions of at least Catholic Christianity.[12] Durkheim was not so positive. For him, a major task of the state is to free individuals from partial societies, such as families, religious collectives, and labor and professional groups. Modern individualism, Durkheim argues, depends on preventing the absorption of individuals into secondary or mediating groups. In antiquity, religious and political institu-

10. *Voltaire's Notebooks,* ed. Theodore Testerman, 2 vols. (Geneva: Institut et Musée, 1952), 2:375ff.

11. John Stuart Mill, *Nature and Utility of Religion* (New York: The Liberal Arts Press, 1958).

12. "Plan of the Scientific Operations Necessary for Reorganizing Society," *On Intellectuals,* ed. Philip Rieff (Garden City, N.Y.: Doubleday, 1969).

tions were but parts of a whole social fabric, an organized social life to which men could not but conform. It is, says Durkheim, only in modern circumstances, brought about by the centralization of government, that individuals acquire personal freedom.[13]

In the twentieth century and on this side of the Atlantic, John Dewey reflects the views of both Mill and Durkheim. Dewey has no use for religion or religious institutions, whatever roles they may have played in the past. Religion is an unreliable source for knowledge and, in spite of contentions to the contrary, even for motivation. Many of the values held dear by the religious are worthy of consideration and they should not be abandoned, but a proper rationale ought to be sought for those deemed commendable. The thrust of Dewey's critique of religion is not merely to eliminate the churches from political life, but to reduce their effectiveness as agencies in private life. Religion is deemed socially dangerous insofar as it gives practical credence to a divine law and attempts to mold personal or social conduct in conformity with norms that look beyond temporal society.[14]

It is in this context that Maritain sets down his reflections on church and state. Although he was a Frenchman, his positions were formed largely by the American context. The principal sources for his views are *True Humanism, Christianity and Democracy, Reflections on America,* and the six lectures he gave at the University of Chicago in 1949, subsequently published as *Man and the State.*[15] Maritain should be read in the company of two junior colleagues

13. Emile Durkheim, *The Elementary Forms of Religious Life,* trans. J. W. Swain (New York: Collier, 1961).

14. See John Dewey, *A Common Faith* (New Haven: Yale University Press, 1934); also Jude P. Dougherty, "Dewey and the Value of Religion," *New Scholasticism,* 51 (1977): 303–27.

15. Jacques Maritain, *Humanisme intégral,* trans. as *True Humanism* (New York: Scribner's, 1938); *Christianity and Democracy* (London: Geoffrey Bles, 1945); *Reflections on America* (New York: Scribner's, 1958); and *Man and the State* (Chicago: University of Chicago Press, 1951).

whom he influenced deeply, namely, Yves Simon and John Courtney Murray, and, one must add, the influence was reciprocal.

In the Chicago lectures Maritain makes a number of distinctions which enable him to deal quickly with some of the issues
raised in the above historical sketch. These distinctions are not
original to Maritain, but they serve to organize some of the elements of the discussion. The most basic is that between "community" and "society."[16] A community, as defined by Maritain, is a
natural structure, having its basis in regional, ethnic, linguistic
or class affinities. Societies, on the other hand, are deliberately
brought into being as their members organize to achieve agreed-
upon ends. Examples of societies are structures such as business
corporations, labor unions, and professional associations. In a
community, in contrast to a society, social relations proceed from
given historical situations and environments; collective patterns of
feeling have the upper hand over personal consciousness, and the
individual appears as the product of the social group. But in a society, personal consciousness and leadership are foremost. Societies
are shaped by individuals. The family is notably one such society.
Though it is the outcome of natural forces, it is fundamentally the
product of personal decisions. A society, observes Maritain, always
gives rise to communities and community feelings within or
around itself. A community, however, is not likely to develop into a
society, though it can be the natural soil from which some societal
organization springs up through reason.

With this understanding of community and society Maritain
can say the nation is a community, not a society. The nation is
something ethico-social; it is a human community based on the
fact of birth and lineage. "An ethnic community, generally speaking, can be defined as a community of patterns of feeling rooted in

16. Maritain, *Man and the State*, 2ff.

the physical soil of the origin of the group as well as in the moral soil of history; it becomes a nation when this factual situation enters the sphere of self-awareness."[17] When the ethnic group becomes conscious of the fact that it constitutes a community of patterns of feeling and possesses its own unity, individuality, and will to endure its existence, then in some sense it becomes a nation. A nation is a community of people, usually with a common language, who have become aware of themselves as history has made them. Put another way, a nation is a community of people who treasure their own past and who love themselves as history has made them. The nation may be said to have a calling.

The nation is not to be confused with the body politic. Nor is the nation to be identified with the state. Maritain finds the notion of "national state" particularly abhorrent.[18] When a state attempts to impose national characteristics, it becomes totalitarian. National community gives rise to political society, but a plurality of national communities can exist within the same body politic. Pre-World War II Germany was a complex of nations which were unable to bring about a genuine body politic. Germany made up for that frustration by an unnatural exaltation of national feeling and the unnatural nation-state. On the other hand, the Austro-Hungarian double crown created a state, but it was unable to produce a nation. France and the United States, says Maritain, have been able to produce a single nation centered on the body politic.

Both the body politic and the state are societies. Though the terms "body politic" and "state" are often used synonymously, they should be distinguished. They differ as whole to part. The body politic is the whole. The primary condition for the existence of the body politic is a common sense of justice, but friendship may be

17. Ibid., 5.
18. Ibid., 7.

said to be its life-giving form. A civic outlook requires a sense of devotion and mutual love as well as a sense of justice and law. These attitudes of mind and will are carried primarily in heritage which itself is preserved by mediating or secondary institutions. Nothing matters more, in the order of material causality, to the life and preservation of the body politic than the accumulated energy and historical continuity of that national community which it has caused to exist. Common inherited experience and moral and intellectual instinct are its basis. Political life and the very existence and prosperity of the body politic depend on the vitality of family, economic, cultural, educational, and religious life.[19]

The state in Maritain's analysis is part of the body politic, that part concerned with the common welfare, the public order, and the administration of public affairs. The state is the part which specializes in the interest of the whole. It is not a man or a body of men but is rather a set of institutions combined into a unified machine. It is made up of experts or specialists in public order and welfare. It constitutes an embodiment of impersonal, lasting superstructure. When functioning properly, it is rational and bound by law. As an instrument of the body politic the state is an agency entitled to use power and coercion. The state is the superior part of the body politic, but it is not superior to the body politic; it exists for man. The state is neither a whole nor a person, nor the subject of a right. The common good of the political society is the final aim of the state and comes before the immediate aim of the state, which is the maintenance of the public order. The special temptation of the state is to exceed its mandate. Power tends to increase power. When it overreaches its mandate, the state tends to ascribe to itself a peculiar common good, namely, its own self-preservation and growth.

19. Ibid., 11.

When the state mistakes itself for the whole of political society and takes upon itself the performance of tasks which normally pertain to the body politic or its organs, we have what Maritain calls the "paternalistic state." From the political point of view, the state is at its best when it is most restrained in seeking the common good. When it takes upon itself the organizing, controlling, or managing of the economic, commercial, industrial, or cultural forms, it has transcended its skill and competence. If the state attempts to become a boss or a manager in business or industry, or a patron of art, or a leading spirit in the affairs of culture, science, and philosophy, it betrays its nature.[20]

The state receives its authority from the body politic, that is, the people. The people have a natural right to self-government. They exercise this right when they establish a constitution, written or unwritten. The people are the multitude of human persons who unite under just laws, by mutual friendship, for their common good. But the people not only constitute a body politic; as human persons they each have a spiritual soul and a supra-temporal destiny. The people are above the state; the people are not for the state, but the state is for the people.

III

Maritain is at pains to emphasize the primacy of the spiritual. From the religious point of view, the common good of the body politic implies an intrinsic though indirect ordination to something which transcends it. In its own order the state is under the command of no superior authority, but the order of eternal life is superior in itself to the order of temporal life. The two orders need not create a conflict. From a secular perspective, the church is an institution concerned with the spiritual in the life of the believer.

20. Ibid., 21.

"From the point of view of the political common good, the activities of the citizens as members of the church have an impact on the common good." Thus the church in one sense is in the body politic, but in another and important sense, she transcends it.[21]

The church and the body politic cannot live and develop in sheer isolation from and ignorance of one another. It is the same human person who is simultaneously a member of the body politic and a member of a church. An absolute division is both impossible and absurd. There must be cooperation. But what form should the cooperation take? It is evident that we no longer live in a sacral age. If classical antiquity or medieval Christianity were characterized by a unity of faith and if that unity of faith was required for a political unity, such does not now seem to be the case. Religious plurality is a fact, and the modern situation seems to demonstrate that religious unity is not a prerequisite for political unity. Nor can the church wield authority over the state, calling emperors, kings, princes, and even entire nations to account. Indeed, the opposite is frequently the case, when the church demands freedom within the political order to develop her own institutions.

The twentieth century has witnessed governments taking upon themselves more and more the role which Tocqueville feared most, namely, that of an immense and tutelary power catering to all needs. In an age of limited government, before government began to play a role in ordering a vast range of social and economic activities, the doctrine of "strict separation" or of "a benevolent neutrality" requiring that the government give no aid of any kind to religion may have made some sense. In an age of positive government, equating neutrality with a strict "no aid" position may be less tenable. The framers of the United States Constitution expected reli-

21. Ibid., 149–52.

gion to play a part in the established social order and also assumed that the state would play a minimal role in forming that order. In our own time, the question of how to treat religious groups and interests has become a fundamentally different one. It can be argued that political equality for religious groups requires that they be able to participate in and have access to the benefits of government programs on the same basis as other groups.

In contrast to the confidence which Mill, Durkheim, and Dewey placed in the dynamism of a secular society, a number of contemporary thinkers have some reservations. It has been suggested that we are only now beginning to understand how intimately and profoundly the vitality of any society is bound up with its religion. Lord Patrick Devlin has argued that the survival of Western culture demands unity as well as freedom. "If men and women try to create a society in which there is no fundamental agreement about good and evil, they will fail; if, having based it on common agreement, the agreement goes, the society will disintegrate."[22] Robert Nisbet speaks of "the pre-democratic state of values and institutions which alone make political freedom possible. To lose, as I believe we are losing, the structure provided by inherited values is surely among the more desolating facts in the present decline of the West."[23] Christopher Dawson maintains that it is the religious impulse which supplies the cohesive force which unifies the society and the culture. The greatest civilizations of the world, Dawson suggests, do not produce the great religions as a kind of cultural by-product; in a very real sense, the great religions are the foundations on which the great civilizations rest.[24] And John Courtney

22. Lord Patrick Devlin, *The Enforcement of Morals* (London: Oxford University Press, 1965),11.

23. Robert Nesbit, *Twilight of Authority* (New York: Oxford University Press, 1979),223.

24. Christopher Dawson, *Religion and the Rise of Western Culture* (New York: Sheed and Ward, 1950), chap. 1.

Murray wrote, "Nothing more imperils both the common good of the earthly city and the supra-temporal interests of truth in human minds than a weakening and breaking down of the internal springs of conscience."[25] In judgments of this sort Maritain would indeed concur. Like Devlin, Nisbet, Dawson, and Murray, he would affirm that much is at stake.

Maritain leaves unresolved the problem of moral unity in a people. He cannot opt for the "common faith," described by John Dewey, a naturalistic credo that goes beyond the merely political, but he is tempted by the "civic faith" delineated by his friend John Courtney Murray in *We Hold These Truths*. But how are the well-springs of conscience and civic faith to be maintained? Before his death Maritain was to see the breakdown of inherited morality on all fronts. A common Christian outlook with respect to matters such as civic decorum, contraception, divorce, abortion, homosexuality, pornography, and capital punishment gave way. The morality commonly affirmed in the nineteenth century came to be denied by great numbers. The denial has been translated into law, if not by legislation then by the courts as they have interpreted the law.

Maritain recognizes that if religious institutions are to possess any authority, it will be the result of moral influence, the result of their being able, through their teachings, to reach the human conscience. Of course, this way of carrying spiritual primacy can be checked by an opposite course of action, chosen by other citizens. But Maritain believes that a free exchange of ideas, despite possible setbacks, is a surer way of attaining influence in the long run. The church is less likely to lose her independence, for if the state is enlisted to implement ecclesiastical goals, the state is likely to serve its

25. John Courtney Murray, *We Hold These Truths* (New York: Sheed and Ward, 1960), 161.

own purposes first. History has taught us that the secular arm is always eager to exercise control, to take the initiative.

Maritain assumes that the church is free to educate and that she is positioned to compete as an equal in the marketplace of ideas. He is conscious that such may not be the actual case, even in the United States which he more or less takes as a paradigm.

The issue is not clear-cut. On the one hand, Maritain affirms that "freedom of inquiry, even at the risk of error, is the normal condition for men to get access to truth, so that freedom to search for God in their own way, for those who have been brought up in ignorance or semi-ignorance of Him, is the normal condition in which to listen to the message of the Gospel."[26] Yet he is convinced, "Willingly or unwillingly States will be obliged to make a choice for or against the Gospel. They will be shaped either by the totalitarian spirit or by the Christian spirit."[27] The West, symbolically at least, continues in many ways to reflect its Christian heritage. Maritain believes that the public acknowledgment of God's existence is good and should be maintained. It is to be expected that a public expression of common faith will assume the form of that Christian confession to which history and the traditions of a people are most vitally linked. As for the citizens who are unbelievers, they will have only to realize that the body politic as a whole is just as free with regard to the public expression of its own faith as they, as individuals, are free with regard to the private expression of their own nonreligious conviction.[28]

In discussing the beneficent influence of religion, Maritain does not confuse morality and religion. The essence of religion for Maritain is, as it was for Augustine and Aquinas, primarily worship. Worship is a species of justice, the paying of a debt to God. Fur-

26. Maritain, *Man and the State*, 161–62.
27. Ibid., 159.
28. Ibid., 172–73.

thermore, morality does not conceptually depend on religion. Moral norms have a life of their own, independent of religion. This is not to say that the religious mind is confined to the endorsement of secular morality. Morality is in many respects changed within a theistic context. Obligations toward God as well as men are recognized. Within Christianity, in particular, suffering and death take on a meaning which they do not have within a secular context. An ascetic life of renunciation, or one of sacrifice, acquires a value which it would not have within a purely materialistic order. A conception of God as personal and loving has implications; only then do prayer and contemplation become habits of mind to be recommended. In the face of adversity, a religious outlook can inspire hope, and holding out a promise of eternal reward for actions that bear no temporal fruit. Christianity counsels patience, love, understanding, long-suffering and humility. Some, but not all of these, conflict with a purely secular outlook.[29]

Other contributions with which Maritain credits religion may be noted. One of the most important is the very one which Durkheim feared. The church, even in a religiously plural society, can stand between the government and the individual, providing a buffer between the two. Religious organizations perform this function by serving the individual in need and by preventing him from becoming completely dependent upon the state for every material necessity. In education and in the care of the sick, the orphaned, and the elderly, the religious institution can provide a type of help that respects the dignity of the person and that responds to individual requirements in a way that often eludes the best-intentioned state institution.[30]

Other subtle but important side effects of a religious outlook include an historical sense and, if you will, a metaphysical sense.

29. Ibid., 176ff.
30. Ibid., 178–79.

Through his religion, the believer is led to identify not simply with a present community of believers, but with a community that has a history, a community that, in some cases, is thought to have been the recipient of a divine revelation. A religious people has a history, and the informed religious mind will attempt to capture that history in order to understand the forces which have shaped the message to which he is heir. The Jew, the Christian, and the Moslem all believe that they are in some sense God's chosen, that something has been revealed to them that has been denied to others. That revelation took place in time. In recapturing that time, the believer transcends his own period. Since sacral history is bound up with secular history, it is more than religious history that will command his attention.[31]

As to the metaphysical sense, the religious mind finds it impossible to discuss the content of its belief without invoking the categories of being. Jerusalem must borrow from Athens. The religious mind also has a sense for order. Nature is regarded as intelligible because it is the handiwork of the divine. It is not by accident that the modern university was born in a religious setting where there was the dual confidence in being's intelligibility and in man's ability to know, attended by further conviction that nature was there to be used for the benefit of man. These were no mean insights, and were to play major roles in the development of Western science and technology.[32]

Certain iconoclasts notwithstanding, religion also carries with it an appreciation for symbol. Religious ritual is one obvious form, employing a multiplicity of symbols. Religious literature is full of

31. Maritain expands this notion in a chapter entitled "Evangelical Inspiration and the Secular Conscience," *Christianity and Democracy*, 27ff.

32. There is a passage in which Maritain speaks of the common good of intellects, "the intelligible treasure of culture in which minds communicate with one another." "It is better," he says "to have Plato, Aristotle, Kant and St. Thomas than to have St. Thomas alone." *Person and the Common Good* (London: Geoffrey Bles, 1948), 58.

metaphor. Because of the ineffable character of that of which religion must speak, simile, allegory, and parables are second nature. The tendency to relate all things to God, to sanctify human acts and occasions, has created not only some of the most delightful feasts of the year, but some of the greatest painting and music and literature the world has known.[33]

Furthermore, it makes a difference whether things are referred to God or not. As many have seen, in a secular society the citizen's rights can only be the social compact of this society. But if rights are looked upon as God-given, if the state itself is accountable to a divine order of things, if civil law is not final, the quality of society can be quite different. The "divine right of kings" doctrine, so happily seized by Western monarchs, was in fact recognized as a Christian heresy. No medieval Christian king could subscribe to the notion that law came from him. Rather, he recognized that his will was subordinate to divine law and that his acts would be judged against a standard not of his making. The notion of God-given rights was taken for granted in the early days of our Republic.

Finally, religion forces man to ask important questions, questions such as what is the purpose of life? What is man's ultimate destiny? What goods are indispensable? How should man behave toward himself, toward his neighbor, toward other peoples, toward nature? What should he consecrate? In raising these questions, religion stimulates a debate which is fruitful, even by its own right, when it produces a Voltaire. As DeGaulle said of Sartre vis-à-vis the latter's contribution to France, "Sartre, he too serves."

If Maritain has a fault, it lies in his idealism, in his optimism that good will and common sense will prevail and that public assessments of the value of religion will result in conclusions similar to those reached by him, conclusions which he believes have been

---

33. See Jacques Maritain "On Artistic Judgment," *The Range of Reason* (New York: Scribner's, 1952), 19ff.

reached by reflective men in every period of the history of the West. Maritain may also be accused of a somewhat romantic view of the United States. He seemed to ignore the fact that manifestations of religion are multifarious and not all beneficent. Few religious bodies possess the high intellectual and cultural tone which Comte prescribed for his ideal society. If assessors of the value of religion are not of one mind as they measure its contributions to the social order, the fault may lie in part with the division and feebleness of religious witness and institutions themselves. Religion seems more to follow than to lead, to sanction what is rather than to inspire. But even if this jaundiced view rather than Maritain's is correct, the question still needs to be raised, what should be the state's attitude toward religion? If social observers are right in decrying a loss of a common, largely a religious, way of looking at things, then an assessment of this social fact ought to be made a public affair. It cannot be assumed that religion's loss of cultural influence, or outright demise, is a social good.

IV

Maritain's contribution to the debate is an analysis which shows religion's indispensable function in society and the concomitant obligation of the state to provide an impartial and unencumbered aid to ensure enlightened internal development within religious bodies, development which alone makes possible a superior cultural contribution. Maritain's genius lies in his appropriation of a tradition that has its roots in the Gospels but one which has developed through twenty centuries in the West. It is a tradition which recognizes two orders, a natural hierarchy between them, and the need for the common good of society to prevail when inevitable tensions arise. While political contexts vary, man is by nature a citizen of two cities. That government is best which recognizes this fact and impedes growth in neither domain.

MARITAIN AT THE CLIFF'S EDGE

From *Antimoderne* to *Le Paysan*

I

Jacques Maritain's was an "engaged" intellect from the very beginning of his academic career. Never one to waffle or to avoid conflict, Maritain joined issue with some of the leading philosophers of his generation. He proved to be an intractable critic of modernity. Maritain was not alone in viewing the dominant philosophy of his day as a danger to Christian belief and practice. Informed Protestants and Catholics on both sides of the Atlantic evaluated nineteenth-century intellectual currents in much the same way. To see this, one has only to contrast the course of American idealism in the last quarter of the nineteenth century with the simultaneous appearance of the Thomistic revival on the European continent.

In the second year of his pontificate, on August 4, 1879, Leo XIII promulgated the encyclical *Aeterni patris,* which endorsed a fledgling Thomistic movement that was to enlist some of the best minds of the following generation. That encyclical was followed by the founding of philosophical institutes at Louvain and Washington for the purpose of making available the thought of St. Thomas as an antidote to the then dominant positivisms and materialism.

The Institut Superiéur de philosophie under the direction of Désiré J. Mercier came into being in 1891; the School of Philosophy at The Catholic University of America under the direction of Edward A. Pace in 1895. The Institute Catholique de Paris was already twelve years old when Leo became Pope and in due course it was to play an important role in the Thomistic revival. Jacques Maritain was to be offered a professorship there in 1914.

Leo recommended to the Catholic world the study of St. Thomas because of the perceived value of his philosophy in meeting "the critical state of the times in which we live." Leo saw that the regnant philosophies of his day not only undercut the faith but also were beginning to have disastrous effects on personal and communal life. Succinctly he says in *Aterni patris*, "Erroneous theories respecting our duty to God and our responsibilities as men, originally propounded in philosophical schools, have gradually permeated all ranks of society and secured acceptance among the majority of men."[1]

Leo recognized that some philosophies opened out to the faith, just as some philosophies closed it off as an intellectual option. Immanuel Kant may be the perfect philosopher for a fideistic form of Protestantism, but he can never become an adequate guide for the Catholic mind. With his dictum, "I have therefore found it necessary to deny knowledge in order to make room for faith,"[2] he reflects the tradition of Luther and Calvin, whose doctrine of original sin holds that with "the fall" intellect is so darkened that it cannot unaided conclude to the existence of God. Catholic thought, by contrast, is essentially and historically a system of intellectualism, of objectivism. The basic principle of Catholic

---

1. Maritain reproduces this encyclical in his *Le doctur angelique* (1930); trans. J. F. Scanlan, *St. Thomas Aquinas: Angel of the Schools* (London, Sheed and Ward, 1948), ix–x.

2. Immanuel Kant, *Critique of Pure Reason*, preface to second edition, trans. Norman Kemp Smith (New York: St. Martin's Press, 1965), 29.

thought asserts the reliability of intelligence, that is, that we are equipped with intellects that are able to know objective reality. Upon the reliability of our knowledge depend our practical decisions, our conduct. We can only do what is right on the condition that we know what is right. We can only live Catholic lives on the condition that we know what Catholic doctrine is.

By any measure, the nineteenth century was no less an intellectually tumultuous one for Europe than the twentieth. Dominated in the intellectual order by the Enlightenment, Anglo-French and German, Europe underwent a systematic attempt on the part of the intelligentsia to replace the inherited, largely classical and Christian learning, by a purely secular ethos. The Napoleonic wars in their aftermath added materially to the destabilization, eradicating many institutional structures: economic and social as well as religious.

Startling advances in the physical sciences reinforced the Enlightenment's confidence in natural reason. In retrospect we can see that the ideas which formed the secular outlook of the nineteenth century were the product of two major intellectual revolutions. The first is associated with the biological investigations of the period and with the names of Spencer, Darwin, Wallace, Huxley and Haeckel. Their work employed the vocabulary of "evolution," "change," "growth," and "development" and led to the worship of progress. The effect of the new biological studies was to place man and his activity wholly in the setting of a natural environment, giving them a natural origin and a natural history. Man was transformed from a being with a spiritual component and a transcendent end, elevated above the rest of nature, into a purely material organism forced to interact within a natural environment like any other living species.

The second revolution resulted from advances in physics that were taken to be a reinforcement of the fundamental assumptions of a mechanistic interpretation of nature. Convinced that all natural phenomena can be explained by structural and efficient causes, the disciples of Locke and Hume discarded any explanation invoking the concepts of "purpose" or "final cause." This convergence of the concepts of physics and biology made possible the resurgence of a purely materialistic concept of man and nature with no need for the hypothesis of a creative God or of a spiritual soul. The foremost symbol of the new outlook became Charles Darwin's *Origin of the Species* (1859). For an intellectual class it codified a view which had been germinating since the preceding century. Darwin confidently marshaled evidence and systematically formulated in a scientific vocabulary ideas already known, but the spontaneous acceptance of his doctrine of evolutionary progress was possible only because the philosophical groundwork had been laid by the Enlightenment fathers.

Leo XIII was not alone in his assessment of the situation. On both sides of the Atlantic various philosophical idealisms were created in a defensive effort to maintain the credibility of religious witness. Challenged by purely naturalistic interpretations of faith, many found the rational support they needed as believers in a post-Kantian idealism. *The Journal of Speculative Philosophy*, the first journal of philosophy in the English language, was founded at St. Louis, Missouri in 1867, the same year that the Institute Catholique de Paris was created, for the dual purpose of making available the best of German philosophy and of providing the Americans with a philosophical forum. In the first issue of the journal, William Torrey Harris gave three reasons for the pursuit of speculative philosophy. In his judgment, speculative philosophy provides, first, a philosophy of religion much needed at a time when traditional religious teaching and ecclesiastical authority are losing their influence. Secondly, it provides a social philosophy compatible with a communal outlook as opposed to a socially devastating individualism. Thirdly, while taking cognizance of the startling advances in the natural sciences, it provides an alternative to empiricism as a philosophy of knowledge. Speculative philosophy for Harris is the tradition beginning with Plato, a tradition which finds its full expression in the system of Hegel.

Josiah Royce (1855–1916) became the most prominent of the American idealists. It is difficult to determine when Josiah Royce first read *Aterni patris,* but twenty-four years after it was published he wrote a laudatory essay entitled, "Pope Leo's Philosophical Movement and Its Relation to Modern Thought."[3] At the height of a distinguished career at Harvard University, Royce was invited to give the Gifford Lectures, 1900–1901. Published as *The World and the Individual,* they attempted to provide a rational basis for religion and morality. In those lectures Royce defended the possibility of truth against the skeptic and the reality of the divine against the agnostic. Royce had little respect for blind faith. He regarded the problem created by Kant's destruction of metaphysics as fundamental. In 1881, he wrote, "we all live, philosophically speaking, in a Kantian atmosphere."[4] Eschewing the outright voluntarism of Schopenhauer, he sought a metaphysics that would permit him to rationally embrace his Christian heritage. Whereas his colleague, William James, was convinced that every demonstrative rational approach to God must fail, Royce was convinced that speculative reason gives one access to God. He thought that the code words of the day, "evolution," "progress," "illusion," "higher criticism," "communism" and "socialism" evoked a mental outlook which reduces Christianity to metaphor and Christian organizations to welfare dispensaries.

Royce saw that the problem was not simply a philosophical one.

3. *The Boston Evening Transcript* (July 29, 1903), Reprinted in Josiah Royce *Fugitive Essays* (Cambridge: Harvard University Press, 1925), 408–29.

4. For an overview of Royce's thought, cf. Bruce Kuklick, *Josiah Royce: An Intellectual Biography* (New York; The Bobbs-Merrill Co., Inc., 1972).

The philosophers tutored the architects of the new biblical criticism, the *Redaktionsgeschichte* movement. David Friedrich Strauss, in his *Das Leben Jesu,* under the influence of Hegel, examined the Gospels and the life of Jesus from the standpoint of the higher criticism and concluded that Christ was not God but a supremely good man whose moral imperative deserved to be followed. This, Royce could not accept; there was no philosophically compelling reason to embrace a purely naturalistic interpretation of the scriptures. Like Leo, he recognized that philosophy must be fought by philosophy.

II

Jacques Maritain was born a generation after Royce and just three years after *Aeterni patris.* By the time Maritain discovered St. Thomas, the Thomistic movement was well under way. It was a movement that not only nourished his searching intellect but one which he substantially enriched. He came to Thomas, he would say, already a Thomist without knowing it. Maritain's influence eventually extended worldwide, notable to Italy, to Latin America, especially Argentina, and to North America.

The convert early on placed his intellect in the service of the church. He knew first hand the contemporary intellectual mileau and shared Leo's assessment of the dominant philosophies that were clearly at odds with the Catholic faith. "If I am anti-modern, it is certainly not out of personal inclination, but because the spirit of all modern things that have proceeded from the anti-Christian revolution compels me to be so, because it itself makes opposition to the human inheritance its own distinctive characteristic, because it hates and despises the past and worships itself . . ."[5]

---

5. Jacques Maritain, *De l'Église du Christ: la personne de l'Église et son personnel;* trans. J W. Evans, *On the Church of Christ: the Person of the Church and Her Personnel* (Notre Dame: University of Notre Dame Press, 1973).

Maritain's critique of Luther, Descartes, and Rousseau, and his early critique of his mentor Henri Bergson, display an intellect fully aware of the impact of ideas and philosophical systems on the practical order. Much of that early work would not today withstand professional scrutiny, largely because of its apologetic character but also because it was often marred by a vagueness and imprecision which his critics easily exploited. Furthermore, Maritain did not in practice always keep clear the distinction between philosophy and theology. It made him later an easy target for American philosophers schooled in the prevailing pragmatic naturalism, such as Sidney Hook and Ernest Nagel. It also hurt his chance for an appointment at the University of Chicago. Robert M. Hutchins, as president of the University of Chicago, three times tried to get Maritain appointed to its faculty of philosophy. The department blocked the appointment each time, even when Hutchins offered to pay his salary from non-departmental funds, because in the words of one member of the department, "Maritain is a propagandist." Hutchins shot back, "You are all propagandists." On another occasion he sent an emissary, probably John Nef, to the chairman of the department, a well-known positivist. The response to Hutchins was, "Maritain is not a good philosopher." The emissary then asked, "Do you have any good philosophers on your faculty?" The answer, "No, but we know what a good philosopher is."[6]

As a critic of modernity Maritain was at times violent and cutting. Raïssa was to say of his style, "As for the men whose ideas he criticized, he certainly respected them personally, but they were for him scarcely more than vehicles for abstract doctrines."[7] Etienne Gilson, when asked by a journalist to comment on the difference

6. Cf. Milton Mayer, *Robert Maynard Hutchins: A Memoir* (Berkeley: University of California Press, 1993,) 118.

7. Jacques Maritain, *Memoirs*, 353, as quoted by D. and I. Gallagher, *The Achievement of Jacques and Raïssa Maritain*, (Garden City, NY: Doubleday, 1962), 12.

between his method and that of Maritain, characterized Maritain's as one that sets bare ideas in juxtaposition, submerging the individuality of the philosophers who espoused them. Speaking of his own technique, Gilson said, "It is more important to try to understand ideas through men . . . in order to judge in a way that unites. . . . Pure ideas, taken in their abstract rigor are generally irreconcilable."[8] But Maritain was not put off. His response: "It is not psychology, but the critique of philosophers which brings truth to light." Where truth is concerned there can be no compromise. One ought to be tenderhearted and tough-minded, not hardhearted and softheaded. Yet Maritain could say, "I am content to owe something to Voltaire in what concerns civil tolerance, and to Luther in what concerns non-conformism, and to honor them in this." In *Theonas* he acknowledges a respect for Comte insofar as he seeks the realization of human order, for Kant for the restoration of the activity of the knowing subject, and for Bergson for the recognition of the spiritual.[9]

It is commonly acknowledged that Maritain's best work in the area of social and political philosophy was accomplished during his years in America. What gives that work power, however, is its grounding in a solid metaphysics of being and in a realistic epistemology. Maritain the metaphysician is at his best in his *A Preface to Metaphysics* and in his *Existence and the Existent*. As a theorist of knowledge he produced *The Degrees of Knowledge, Philosophy of Nature,* and *Creative Intuition in Art and Poetry*. With the exception of the last mentioned, those works formed the background to his political philosophy, a political philosophy that had considerable influence on important thinkers such as Mortimer Adler, John

8. Laurence K. Shook, *Etienne Gilson* (Toronto, Pontifical Institute of Medieval Studies, 1984), 194.

9. Jacques Maritain, *Theonas*, trans. F. J. Sheed (New York: Sheed and Ward, 1933), 172.

Courtney Murray, and Yves Simon and on more than one generation of Thomists who staffed the then flourishing Catholic colleges
and universities in the United States. Many students were first ex-
posed to philosophy through his clearly written *Introduction to
Philosophy.*

III

It is Maritain's recognition of the practical effects of the materialisms and empircisms of his day and his critique of the Enlightenment spirit which is the focus of this inquiry. One of his earliest
works sets the tone for much that is to come. The myth of "necessary progress" as found in philosophers like Condorcet and Comte
is one of his major targets in *Theonas,* a dialogue first published in
1921. He quotes Condorcet, "There will then come a moment upon
this earth when the sun will shine on none but free men who recognize no other master than their reason; when tyrants and slaves,
priests and their stupid hypocritical instruments, will exist no
more save in history and on the stage."[10] And Auguste Comte, "To
re-establish the Catholic order it would be necessary to suppress
the philosophy of the eighteenth century, and as this philosophy
proceeds from the Reformation, and Luther's Reformation in its
turn was but the result of the experimental sciences introduced
into Europe by the Arabs, it would be necessary to suppress the sciences."[11] Maritain, through the character Theonas, responds to
Comte as follows: "That surely is a perfect text, I know it by heart:
and it illustrates as clearly as the historico—economic syntheses of
Karl Marx—what havoc the myth of progress can work in the
mind of an intelligent man."[12]

As Maritain characterizes it, "the law of progress" demands the

---

10. Ibid., 117.   11. Ibid., 126.
12. Ibid., 126–27.

ceaseless changing of foundations and principles inherited from the past; but if foundations can change, that which rests on them must also change. The movement of humanity towards the better, according to this attitude, demands the regular destruction of all previous gains. The progressivists, says Maritain, fail to recognize that there are types of change. Some can be constructive, as Thomas in building upon Augustine. The truths of Ptolemaic astronomy survive in the Copernican revolution. The production of a plant is bound up with the corruption of the seed. "There is no destruction," he argues, "that does not produce something, no production that does not destroy some existent thing. The whole question is to know whether it is the production or the destruction which is the principal event."[13] Judgment is required. The conservative takes newness to be a sign of corruption; the mystics of revolution take all newness for a newness of achievement. Placed in perspective, the myths of "humanity," "the city of the future," "revolution" and "necessary progress" are but secular substitutions for Christian ideas such as the "church," the "heavenly Jerusalem," "regeneration" and "providence." When men cease to believe in the supernatural, Maritain says, the Gospel is reduced to the plane of nature.[14]

Although Maritain's early targets are Bergson and the three reformers, the real enemy is Immanuel Kant. In Maritain's judgment, Kant's critical philosophy is born of the convergence of the three intellectual currents represented by 1) Luther's revolt in theology, 2) Descartes' in philosophy, and 3) Rousseau's in ethics. Kant represents a lack of confidence in the intellect's ability to metaphysically grasp being. Bergson similarly underestimates the intellect. Maritain is willing to commended Bergson for attacking

13. Ibid., 137.
14. Ibid., 139–40.

the anti-metaphysical prejudices of nineteenth-century positivism, but in Maritain's judgment Bergson's notion of "intuition" and his theory of conceptual knowledge leads, not unlike Descartes, to a subjectivism and irrationalism. In retrospect, we can see that Maritain may have more in common with Bergson than not; nevertheless, he saw the difficulty of maintaining an objectivist metaphysics and even natural science on Bergson's somewhat anti-intellectualist epistemology. In Maritain's judgment, both Bergson and Kant give too large a role to the activity of the experiencing subject in constituting the known. Maritain's conviction that the realism of Aristotle and Aquinas is perfectly in accord with common sense and with modern science finds full expression in his mature work, *The Degrees of Knowledge*.[15]

Maritain's notion of philosophy is important. "Modern philosophies" he writes, "grow out of what has gone before, but rather by way of contradiction; the Scholastics by way of agreement and further development." The result is that philosophy in our day is like a series of episodes simply stuck end to end, not like a tree where each branch is organically related to each and all to the roots.[16] "The labor of the mind, by its very nature demands a collaboration running through the years." There is such a thing as a *philosophia perennis;* though its source is in antiquity, it is forever open-ended.

IV

In the closing years of his life Maritain returned to themes which he first approached as a young convert to the Catholic faith, grateful for the insight provided by his newly acquired faith. In the

---

15. Jacques Maritain, *Distinguer pour unir; ou les degrés du savior* (1932), trans. B. Wall and M. Adamson, *The Degrees of Knowledge,* (London: Geoffrey Bles, Century Press, 1937).

16. Maritain, *Theonas,* 5.

last decade of his life, the old philosopher, equipped with both the faith and years of experience, reflected at length on the condition of his beloved Catholic Church. Between 1966 and 1973 he produced three books. One may view these simply as works of apologetics, but one may also find in them profound philosophical insight. The most widely noted was his *Paysan de la Garonne* published in 1966 shortly after the close of the Second Vatican Council when Maritain was eighty-four years of age. *On the Grace and Humanity of Christ* appeared in 1969; *On The Church of Christ* followed four years later.

Acknowledging that he was writing in a "troubled historical moment," Maritain presents *On the Church of Christ* as a reflection of a philosopher on the faith accorded him through the instrument of the Church. The book, he proclaims, is not a work of apologetics; "It presupposes the Catholic faith and addresses itself above all to Catholics, (and) to our nonseparated brothers who recite the Credo each Sunday."[17] It addresses itself to others to the extent that they "desire to know what Catholics believe even if the latter seem sometimes to have forgotten it."[18]

The last is not an idle remark. In Maritain's judgment, Vatican II unleashed a subversive movement in the Church which constitutes perhaps an even greater threat to her integrity than the external modernist attack of the nineteenth century. "The modernism of Pius X's time," he writes, was "only a modest hay fever" compared to the sickness which besets the intellectuals today.[19] In *Le Paysan*, he speaks of an "immanent apostasy." The new theologians through an exhausting work of "hermeneutic evacuation" have

17. Jacques Maritain, *De l'Église du Christ* (1973), trans. J. W. Evans, *On the Church of Christ* (Notre Dame: University of Notre Dame Press, 1973), vi.

18. Ibid.

19. Jacques Maritain, *Paysan de la Garonne* (1966), trans. M. Cuddihy and E. Hughes, *The Peasant of the Garonne,* (New York: Holt, Rinehart, and Winston, 1968), 14.

emptied our faith of every specific object and reduced it to a "simple sublimating aspiration." "The frenzied modernism of today is incurably ambivalent. Its natural bent, although it would deny it, is to ruin the Christian faith."[20] Ironically, Maritain says, the leaders of our neo-modernism declare themselves Christian, even though they have separated themselves from its basic tenets. In a way, their attitude is a backhanded compliment to Christianity itself, insofar as they still cherish their identification with the Church.

Maritain asks, "if divine transcendence is only the mythical projection of a certain collective fear experienced by man at a given moment in history," then why should an observer faithful to the tradition "be astonished that so many modernists believe they have a mission to save a dying Christianity, their dying Christianity for the modern world."[21] Simply put, modernism and Christianity are incompatible.

A Greek confidence in the human intellect and the intelligibility of nature is the cornerstone of Maritain's philosophy of being. It led him, on first acquaintance, to an appreciation of the realism of St. Thomas whom he came to venerate both as a person and as a philosopher/theologian. Even before the end of the Second Vatican Council, Maritain sadly detects a drift away from St. Thomas on the part of Catholic theologians. The symptoms are many. He finds that all too often references to St. Thomas and the Scholastics are made in a disparaging tone. The call to de-Hellenize Christianity, he is convinced, is usually a repudiation of philosophical realism and the first step toward a subjectivism which reduces the revealed word of God to mere symbols for truths accessible to human reason. He finds this regrettable not only because it repudiates a great teacher but because of its implications for theology

20. Ibid., 17.
21. Ibid., 19.

as a discipline. Theology, heretofore, was thought of as "rational knowledge." The new approach, by contrast, when it does not reduce the faith to *praxis,* seems to adopt a fideistic starting point. Christ is the way, if one is inclined to adopt Him as a starting point. In an aside, Maritain notes "some of our well-bred contemporaries are repelled by the vocabulary of Aquinas." Yet it is hard to believe that men who understand Hegel, Heidegger, and Jean-Paul Sartre should be terrorized by scholastic terminology. They should know perfectly well that every science has its technical vocabulary.[22] Their difficulty lies much deeper, in the skepticisms they have unwittingly embraced, skepticisms which deny the intellect's ability to reach being in knowledge and speech. The only way we can logically and clearly express many of the truths of the faith is by appropriating the language of ontology. If we cannot know reality in itself but only as it appears to us, what are we to make of the teachings of Chalcedon, i.e., that Jesus Christ is one person with two natures, one divine and one human? What are we to make of the doctrine of the Eucharist, that Christ is physically present under the appearance of bread and wine?

Speaking of method, the teaching of Aquinas, "it is not the doctrine of one man, but the whole labor of the Fathers of the Church, the seekers of Greece . . . the inspired of Israel"[23] and the scholars of the medieval Arabic world. Far from reaching a dead-end, the Thomistic corpus "is an intelligible organism meant to keep on growing always, and to extend across the centuries its insatiable thirst for new prey. It is a doctrine open and without frontiers; open to every reality wherever it is and every truth from wherever it comes, especially the new truth which the evolution of culture or science will enable it to bring out."[24] It is, too, a doctrine open to

22. Ibid., 155.　　　　　　　23. Ibid., 153.
24. Ibid.

the various problematics it may see fit to employ, whether created from within or adopted from without. Because it is an open doctrine, it is indefinitely progressive. Those who adopt the philosophy of St. Thomas recognize that their master does not require subservience. "The philosopher swears fidelity to no person, nor any school—not even if he be a Thomist—to the letter of St. Thomas and every article of his teaching."[25]

Josiah Royce saw this more than a half century earlier. Writing as an outsider, he was convinced that the neo-scholastic movement endorsed by Leo XIII was an important one, in Royce's words, "for the general intellectual progress of our time." The use of St. Thomas, he says, entails growth, development and change. He even uses the word "progress." "Pope Leo, after all, 'let loose a thinker' amongst his people—a thinker to be sure, of unquestioned orthodoxy, but after all a genuine thinker whom the textbooks had long tired, as it were to keep lifeless, and who, when once revived, proves to be full of the suggestion of new problems, and of an effort towards new solutions."[26] But Royce was also fearful that a resurgent Thomism might give way to the Kantian legions and their demand that the epistemological issue be settled first. In Maritain he would have found a kindred spirit.

The key to Maritain's conception of philosophy, his love for St. Thomas, and his chagrin at contemporary drifts in theology is grounded, as I said, in his doctrine on being. "To maintain . . . that the object of our intellect is not the being of things but the *idea* of being which it forms in itself, or more generally that we apprehend immediately only our ideas, is to deliver oneself bound hand and foot to skepticism."[27] Maritain's controlling principle can be stated

25. Ibid., 161.

26. Royce, *Fugitive Essays*, 422–23.

27. Jacques Maritain, *Eléménts de philosophie*, trans. E. I. Watkin, *Elements of Philosophy;* (New York: Sheed and Ward, 1930), 186.

simply: being governs inquiry. There are structures apart from the mind which can be objectively grasped. Or put another way, being is intelligible. And not only being, but being in act is intelligible. The senses bring us into contact with a material, changing world but in the flux of events there are identifiable structures which control enquiry. Although the senses are limited to the material singular, there is more in the sense report than the senses themselves are formally able to appreciate. The intellect's ability to abstract enables it to grasp the universal, the intelligible nature, the "whatness" of the thing. Those things that are not self-intelligible need to be explained by means of things other than themselves.[28] Thus, acknowledging the principles of substance and causality, Maritain avoids the phenomenalism of Locke and the empiricism of Hume. So equipped, he is able to reason to an immaterial order and to the existence of God, *ipsum esse subsistens.* Maritain's defense of the first principles of thought and being in his little book, *A Preface to Metaphysics,* is difficult to surpass.

Philosophies which fail to achieve a doctrine of being will inevitably be subjective in tone. Methodologically, they will be cut off from the transcendent source of being itself. Oddly, philosophy seems to entail a theology whether it reaches God or not. "When Feuêrbach declared that God was the creation and the alienation of man; when Nietzsche proclaimed the death of God, they were the theologians of our contemporary atheistic philosophies."[29] They define themselves and their projects against a tradition they hope to supersede, but one in which their own roots are planted.

---

28. Jacques Maritain, *Court traité de l'existence et de l'existant* (1947), trans. L. Galantière and G. B. Phelan, *Existence and the Existent* (New York: Pantheon, 1948), 10–46; *Sept leçons sur l'être et les Premieres Principes de la Raison Speculative* (1934), trans. B. Wall, *A Preface to Metaphysics* (New York: Sheed and Ward, 1948), lectures II–IV, 43–89.

29. Maritain, *Existence and the Existent,* 137.

"Why are these philosophies so charged with bitterness," Maritain asks, "unless it is because they feel themselves chained in spite of themselves to a transcendence and to a past they constantly have to kill."[30] Theirs is, in fact, a religious protest in the guise of philosophy.

V

If any conclusion is to be drawn from this, one must acknowledge that the chairman of the philosophy department at the University of Chicago may have had it right when he said, "Maritain is an apologist." He was one all of his professional life. But Maritain was philosophizing within a Thomistic framework where philosophy in the service of theology loses nothing of its integrity. In fact, as Maritain consistently affirmed, the philosopher himself may gain insight by his association with a theological perspective which thrusts new problems and demands greater precision. Maritain maintains that philosophy in the abstract is pure philosophy and can never be "Christian," but concretely it is always pursued within a social setting which in providing a mileau for reflection, gives it color, if not direction. In *Existence and the Existent* he writes that we do not philosophize in the posture of dramatic singularity; we do not save our souls in the posture of theoretic universality and detachment from self for the purpose of knowing.[31] William James and John Dewey could have said as much.

Maritain the young apprentice and Maritain the aging philosopher are not only men of the faith, but are both graced with that prelude to philosophy which we call "common sense." Both are philosophical realists and both respect the claims of revealed truth. Maritain the lecturer at some of North America's most prestigious

30. Ibid.
31. Ibid., 135.

universities, Maritain the signatory of the Declaration of Human Rights, Maritain the Ambassador to the Holy See, all remained in their diverse careers the disciple of Leon Bloy, Henri Bergson and Thomas Aquinas. The aging Maritain may have written a seemingly nostalgic, *Antimoderne,* he may have called himself "Le Paysan," but no historian will ever deny his "engagement" with the leading ideas of his day. Leon Bloy, Maritain's spiritual mentor, called himself, "The Pilgrim of the Absolute"; Maritain, the inveterate foe of anti-intellectualism, could be called the "Pilgrim of the Transcendent."

MARITAIN AS AN INTERPRETER
OF AQUINAS ON THE PROBLEM OF
INDIVIDUATION

I

The medieval problem of individuation is not the contemporary problem of "individuals" or "particulars" discussed by P. F. Strawson, J. W. Meiland, and others.[1] In a certain sense the problem of individuation originates with Parmenides, but it is Plato's philosophy of science which bequeaths the problem to Aristotle and to his medieval commentators. Its solution in Aquinas is not that of Aristotle, nor is it that of Scotus or Suarez. Aquinas will distinguish between the problem of individuation and what we may call the problem of "individuality" or the problem of "subsistence." The solution to both will draw upon many Aristotelian distinctions but will incorporate key elements of St. Thomas's own metaphysics, including the real distinction between essence and existence and his doctrine of participation.

It is Maritain's appropriation of St. Thomas's metaphysics which enables him to produce a realistic philosophy of science, one which

1. Cf. P. F. Strawson, *Individuals: An Essay in Descriptive Metaphysics* (London: Methuen and Co., 1959); J. W. Meiland, *Talking about Particulars* (New York: Humanities Press, 1970); P. Butchvarov, *Resemblance and Identity* (Bloomington: Indiana University Press, 1966).

he offers as compatible with contemporary scientific inquiry. It also enables him to develop a theory of person and personality. But the story begins with Plato.

Although Plato's theory of knowledge may appear fanciful to the modern reader, his analysis of scientific knowledge contains a basic set of observations whose truth remains uncontested even though his explanation be faulty. Plato saw clearly that science is of the universal. Things may be particular, but when we consider them as objects of inquiry, the intellect focuses upon the form taken as an exemplar. In Plato's explanation, things belong to their various kinds by participating in incorporeal, eternal, and unchangeable archetypes. From a realist's vantage point the problem may be stated simply: since things are singular, how is it that we intellectually apprehend them as universal. Aristotle's solution is well known, and it is one adopted and amplified by St. Thomas. Universals are abstracted from singular things.

No one would present Maritain as a medievalist, but as an interpreter of Aquinas he has wielded considerable influence in the United States and in Latin America. Many have come to St. Thomas under his tutelage. His knowledge of Aquinas is extensive and is drawn upon throughout his lifelong work but perhaps nowhere more than in his philosophy of science and in his discussions of the person. The primary text for Thomas's doctrine of individuation is his commentary on Boethius's *De trinitate*, where he discusses the division and methods of the sciences. Maritain's philosophy is indebted mainly to his reading of Thomistic texts, but he draws heavily as well on the works of his contemporaries Reginald Garrigou-Lagrange and Louis Geiger, and on those of the classic commentators on Thomas, Cajetan, Sylvester of Ferrara, and John of St. Thomas.

Alhough employing St. Thomas, Maritain is always a man of the twentieth century. In such books as the *Degrees of Knowledge,*

Science and Wisdom, Existence and the Existent, and *A Preface to Metaphysics* his foe is always some contemporary exponent of a nominalist position.[2] Nominalists, he will say, have a taste for the real, but no sense of being.[3] Timeless metaphysics, he will lament, no longer suits the modern intellect. Three centuries of empirico-mathematics have so warped the intellect that it is no longer interested in anything but the invention of apparatus to capture phenomena.[4] An overstatement to be sure, but indicative of the thrust of Maritain's metaphysical project: to engender a respect for the stable, enduring, timeless aspects of things.

II

My aim in this presentation is first to set forth the Thomistic doctrine and then to speak to Maritain's appropriation of it to show that Thomas is alive in the twentieth century. Within the philosophy of St. Thomas, it is first necessary to distinguish between the problem of "individuation" and the problem of "individuality," although Thomas himself does not use the latter term.[5]

2. Jacques Maritain, *Les Degrés du savoir* (1932), trans. G. B. Phelan from fourth French edition, *Degrees of Knowledge* (New York: Scribner's, 1959); *Science et sagesse* (1935), trans. B. Wall, *Science and Wisdom* (New York: Scribner's, 1940); *Court traité de l'existence et de l'existant* (1947), trans. L. Galantière and G. B. Phelan, *Existence and the Existent* (New York: Pantheon, 1948); *Sept leçons sur l'être et les premières principes de la raison spéculative,* (1934), trans. B. Wall, *A Preface to Metaphysics* (New York: Sheed and Ward, 1948).

3. Maritain, *Degrees of Knowledge,* 3.

4. Ibid.

5. For a discussion of the diverse terminology employed in addressing the problem from the Middle Ages to the present, see Jorge J. E. Gracia, *Introduction to the Problem of Individuation in the Middle Ages* (Washington, D.C.: The Catholic University of America Press, 1984). Other works of interest include, Gracia, *Individuality: An Essay on the Foundations of Metaphysics* (Albany: State University of New York Press, 1988), Gracia, ed., *Individuation and Identity in Early Modern Philosophy* (Albany: State University of New York Press, 1994); Gracia, eds., *Individuation in Scholasticism: The Later Middle Ages and the Counter-Reformation (1150–1650)* (Albany: State University of New York Press, 1994).

Both are aspects of what may be called "the problem of multiplicity and plurality." The distinction of one thing from another is the problem of "individuality" or "subsistence." Membership in the same class is the problem of "individuation." Metaphysical analysis forces us to recognize both. Whereas being is directly attained in a highly individualized manner through judgment, it is conceptualized in the widest of its universal aspects.

As agents reflecting on nature, we are confronted not only with a multitude of individual beings but also with a multitude of beings within a class. Philosophically, how are we to explain numerical differentiation? How, on the other hand, are we to explain the existence of beings which share with each other a distinctive character? Or put another way: from a philosophical point of view, how is the evident individuality of a being maintained at the same time its sameness with others in a class is said to have a foundation in reality? It is axiomatic that where there is similarity we must look for difference lest similarity becomes identity.

Indeed, Plato recognized the problem. To the question how can there be many individuals in a class, each member sharing a limited perfection of the class, his doctrine of forms and his notion of participation supplied the answer. Aristotle's analysis of cognition, his doctrine of abstraction, and his distinction between potency and act provided him with materials for a different answer. For Aristotle, the groupings are not subjective but have a basis in reality. The intellect can consider all members of a class under a single concept because of the process of abstraction in which differences are left aside. Each member of a class has in common with other members of its class a nature, or essence, different from that had in common by the members of other classes. The groupings are not invented by the intellect but are discovered in antecedent reality. Given that analysis, how is sameness between beings which have their own unique reality to be explained?

For Thomas, the context is not simply the Aristotelian one or even the one he encounters in commenting on Boethius's *De trinitate*. Thomas's full explanation will incorporate his doctrine of the real distinction between essence and existence and his notion of participation. Considering the texts of Aquinas, the first aspect of the problem of the one and the many is the multiplication of beings: how can there be more than one being?[6] His distinction between essence and existence, between *what the thing is* and *the act whereby it is,* is crucial. There can be more than one being because the *act of to be* can be limited in a multiplicity of ways. In finite beings essence places a limitation on the act of to be. But individuality is a concept that pertains not only to material natures but to the divine and to angelic natures as well. It is existence that makes one thing distinct from another. ". . . two features belong to the notion of an individual, namely, that it is actually existent, either in itself or in something else; and that it be divided from other things that are or can be in the same species, existing undivided in itself."[7] Those two features, existence-as-a-unit and division from all other things, remain the basic features of Thomas's treatment of individuality. Everything has unity and individuation in accord with its having existence. "Each being" says St. Thomas, "possesses its act of existing and its individuation in accordance with the same factor."[8] But existence cannot give rise to diversity. Plurality requires the recognition of composition. Every being other than subsistent being is necessarily composite, involving its own limitation. Individuality is brought about by something that functions only in a potential not in an actual manner.

In purely spiritual, but nevertheless finite creatures, form is the

---

6. Thomas Aquinas, *Summa Theologiae*, I, 29, 4.
7. Thomas Aquinas, *Sentences* IV, 12, 1, 1, ad 3.
8. Thomas Aquinas, *De Anima* 1, ad 2.

sole essential cause of the individuality of a substance. Each distinctive form, or essence, places a different limitation on its act of to be. Thus Thomas can say that each angel is a species unto itself. With material substances, however, we have individuals, each with its own act of to be, but having a sameness because its nature places on it the same limitation of the act of to be.

To the question "How can there (in the case of material substances) be many similar individuals in a class, each member showing a limited perfection of the class?" Thomas answers that the difference must be caused by something distinctive of matter itself. If each individual is regarded as participating in the perfection possible to its class, the principle of limitation cannot be found in the form, or principle of actuality, which makes the composite thing to be what it is, but only in the potential essence or prime matter. Without such a limiting principle the essence could not be multiplied. Considered abstractly, there is nothing in the concept of "essence" as such which requires multiplication. Conceivably, as with angels, an essence could be a species unto itself. The principle of actuality in the essence, that which makes the thing to be what it is, is the form. For a form to be multiplied, it must be limited. In fact, there is no individual being of our experience which exhausts all the conceivable perfections of its class. Whatever is later to be said about the role of "signate matter," primary matter for Thomas is the first intrinsic potential principle of limitation in the essence of material things. It must be noted that Aristotle's hylomorphic doctrine becomes in the hands of Thomas a metaphysical doctrine and not merely one to explain change.

For Thomas, the problem of individuation is not simply one of how an individual is recognized, i.e., by shape, size, color or activity. Beings, rather, are intrinsically different within their own class. Quantity, on this account, exercises an auxiliary role. On this interpretation, the principle of individuation by which each being is distinct from every other member of its class or species is a physical intrinsic constitutive principle in the individual essence. Whereas Aristotle identifies the individual essence with unchangeable form, Thomas places in material essences themselves an intrinsic principle of limitation, namely, primary matter.

The positions taken by Cajetan, Sylvester of Ferrara and John of St. Thomas constitute alternative interpretations of Aquinas and are responsible for discussions that extend over centuries. Maritain, although indebted to Cajetan in many respects, is closer to Sylvester than to Cajetan in his understanding of the role of "signate matter." Quantity for Thomas is understood as a proper accident inhering in the material substance whereby the substance has parts outside of parts in space, that is, has extension. Matter under determinate dimensions, "signate matter," as a proper accident, flows from the essence necessarily. It may be called an "absolute" or necessary accident. Essentially divisible, quantity is the basis of numerical designation. It makes a material substance fully individuated in a class or species. Yet it should be remembered that, on Thomistic principles, what is primarily individuated is neither the matter nor the form but the received act of to be. Thomas' distinction between the principles of essence and existence, principles related to each other as potency is to act, is thus the foundation of his doctrine of individuation.

Thomas's theory of being is consistent with his theory of knowledge. Whereas Scotus will say, "That which is first known by the intellect is the individual being,"[9] Thomas insists that the intellect does not immediately and directly know the individual as individual but, rather, knows it indirectly and reflectively by a turning back to the image. The Thomistic universal is produced by abstraction, not as Scotus would have it by a process of precision

9. Duns Scotus, John, *Opus Oxoniense*, I, d.3.

or cutting off (abcissus) of differences. The Scotistic theory of individuation is consistent with Scotus's theory of knowledge, but that is another story.

III

Maritain incorporates these doctrines in a well-developed theory of being and knowledge. They play a central role in his philosophy of science, which remains essentially that of St. Thomas but is updated to take account of modern achievements. He draws upon Thomas' theory of abstraction, his doctrine of causality, his theory of explanation and, of course, his solution to the problem of individuation.

Maritain takes as his starting point the manner in which the object of natural science is attained. To use his own language, when the mind's eye falls upon the flux of the sensible, it must immediately turn from it to the intelligible, the immutable, which is able to be extracted by the mind from the things of sensory experience. It is only in the mind that the universal enjoys the positive unity proper to it.[10] Yet the intelligible object as resident in external things and in the senses is a concrete singular. The intelligible instead of being transcendent to things is there immanent in them. The object of science is not an *ens rationis* but the *natures* of material things. The senses reveal ontological diversity and report a multiplicity of happenings in a changing world. The intellect, discerning commonality, moves from an experience of the singular to affirmations about the class. It is those observations, formulated as patterns or laws of nature, which stand in need of explanation. The movement from particular to universal leaves difference behind. It is a characteristic of science, in general, not simply modern mathematical science, to do away with individuation. There can be no

10. Maritain, *Degrees of Knowledge*, 22 ff.

science of the particular and yet the particular cannot be understood without the conceptual schema science brings to it.

"It is absolutely necessary to distinguish the *thing* with which science is concerned . . . and the perfectly precise object, ("the formal object") upon which it lays hold and from which it derives its stability."[11] Anyone beginning in this manner will soon have to confront the problem of individuation. If one begins as a nominalist, one has an entirely different sort of problem, most likely, in contemporary parlance, "the reidentification of particulars." Maritain's starting point is obviously Plato's. "Science," he writes, "bears directly and of itself upon the abstract, on ideal constancies and super momentary determinations—let us say, on the intelligible objects that the mind seeks out in the real and sets free from it. They are there, they exist there, but not at all in the conditions of abstraction and universality that they have in the mind."[12] Human nature is realized concretely in each of us, but only in the mind is it realized as a universal nature common to all men. The laws of nature described by the natural science are possible because they concern natures or essences. Take, for example, the law of expansion of solids by heat. The law means that a solid has within it the secrets of its nature, a certain structure which necessarily and unfailingly determines it to expand according to specific coefficients under the action heat.[13] Heat may be described as kinetic energy and further described in a statistical law governing molecular motion, but behind this statistical law there is a nature which is undergoing modification. Movement is of its very nature a physical and not a mathematical thing. Nominalism of necessity is limited to the sense report and leads to mechanism as a philosophy of sci-

11. Ibid., 24.   12. Ibid.
13. Ibid., 25–26.

ence. "If the universal does not directly or indirectly designate an essence, but only a collection of individual cases, it is not at all possible to understand how scientific law can be necessary and the succession of singular events contingent."[14] The mind can consider intelligible objects abstracted from, and purified of, matter but only to the extent that matter is the basis of diversity amongst individuals within a species, i.e., insofar as matter is a principle of individuation.[15]

Basic to Maritain's understanding of the problem of individuality is Thomas's distinction between essence and existence, between the "whatness" of the thing and the act of "to be" whereby it is. This is seen in Maritain's analysis of the so-called "existential judgment." "In one simultaneous awakening of the intellect and the judgment the intellect affirms the existence of something," i.e., "this thing exists."[16] "In forming this judgment the intellect, on the one hand, knows the subject as singular (indirectly and by reflection upon phantasms) and on the other hand, affirms that this singular subject exercises the act of existence."[17] It thus reaches the *actus essendi* (in judging)—as it reaches essence (in conceiving)—by meditation on sensorial perception.

With respect to self-knowledge the intellect only secondarily, by an explicit reflection upon its own act, becomes conscious of itself as thinking subject. The intellect is ordered primarily to being. From the very beginning, in the act of knowing it knows explicitly as extra-mental, the being and the existence of its object.[18]

14. Ibid., 28–29.
15. Ibid., 35.
16. Maritain, *Existence and the Existent*, 27.
17. Ibid.
18. Ibid., 28.

IV

Maritain's discussion of person is found in a slim but important work, *The Person and the Common Good*. There he draws heavily on St. Thomas, making a distinction between "individuality" and the "person." Both concepts, "individuality" and "person," may be predicated of God, angels, and men. The divine essence in its sovereign unity and simplicity is supremely individual. Angels are individuated essences. In the human composite, individuality flows from the material component. "Matter itself is a kind of nonbeing, a mere potency or ability to receive forms and undergo substantial mutations. . . . In every being made of matter, this pure potency bears the impress of a metaphysical energy—the 'form' or 'soul'—which constitutes with it a substantial unit and determines this unit to be that which it is."[19] Matter is characterized as having an "affinity" for being; it derives all of its determination from form. "By the fact that it is ordained to inform matter, the form finds itself particularized in such and such a being which shares the same specific nature with other beings equally immersed in spatiality."[20] In order to exist, any being must be undivided and distinct from every other existent. In pure spirits individuality derives from the form constituting them as such and giving them their degree of intelligibility. Corporeal beings by contrast are individuated because of matter with its designated quantity. "Their specific form and their essence are not individuated by means of their own entity, but by reason of their transcendental relation to matter understood as implying position in space."[21] As a material entity, man has only a precarious unity, a unity easily shattered

19. Jacques Maritain, *La personne et le bien commun,* trans. J. J. Fitzgerald, *Person and the Common Good* (London: Geoffrey Bles, 1948), 26.
20. Ibid.
21. Ibid., 27.

into a multiplicity, for in itself matter is inclined to disintegration.[22]

The doctrine of participation is invoked, at the same time that the precariousness of human existence is stressed. "As an individual each of us is a fragment of a species, a part of a universe, a unique point in the web of cosmic, ethical, historical forces and influences—and bound by laws. Each of us is subject to the determinism of the physical world."[23] Nonetheless, each of us is a person. Personality signifies interiority, spirituality, and is traceable to the immaterial form. One and the same reality is in one sense an individual and in another sense a person.[24] Our whole being is individual by reason of that in us which derives from matter and is a person by reason of that which derives from spirit.

In another text, speaking of the composite, Maritain writes, "We cannot conceive the notion of body without the notion of organism, of *caro et ossa*, and we cannot conceive the notion of organism without the notion of qualitative heterogeneity; and we cannot conceive the notion of qualitative heterogeneity without that of the properties perceived by the senses."[25]

In this text Maritain is arguing that we must respect the sense report of material reality. Because the sensory properties flow from the essence of the material nature, the senses themselves disclose far more than they are formally able to appreciate. The form or principle of intelligibility is grasped intellectually in the sense report. Respect for simple sense awareness is suppressed in purely physico-mathematical reports dependent on instruments of observation and measurement which methodologically fail to attain the intelligible whole. The universe of abstract quantity, Maritain will say, filters out nature.[26]

22. Ibid.

23. Ibid.

24. Ibid., 31.

25. Maritain, *Science et sagesse*, 57–58.

26. Ibid., 58–59.

Maritain earlier in his *Degrees of Knowledge* laid the groundwork for this analysis of the concept of "person." In that work he uses the word "subsistence" rather than "individuality" in making distinctions. "The first metaphysical root of personality is what is called subsistence. Subsistence presupposes a (substantial) nature that is individual or singular."[27] This nature (person) from the fact that it is endowed with subsistence cannot communicate with any other substantial nature in the very act of existence. It is, so to speak, absolutely enclosed with regard to existence.[28] "Subsistence is for the nature an ontological seal, as it were, of its unity. When this nature is complete (a separated soul is not a person) and above all when it is capable of possessing itself, of taking itself in hand by the intellect and will, in short, when it belongs to the spiritual order, then the subsistence of such a nature is called personality."[29] Man must win his personality as he wins his liberty. A person develops personality within a community and runs the risk of contamination thereby. "For the same man who is a person . . . is also an individual in a species and dust before the wind."[30] Predicated of man, the word "personality" implies the laborious and the limited, the indigent and the complicated. Yet it designates man in the fullness of his human condition.

From considerations of human personality it is possible to free the notion "personality" from material limitation and predicate it not only of man but of angels and of God as well. Of angels, Maritain writes, "Think of what an angelic person must be. Such a one is still a created subject, but each exhausts by himself alone a whole specific essence. Finite in relation to God, he is infinite in relation to us. He subsists immutably above time, a mirror of God and of the universe."[31] And of God, he writes, "In reality, as soon as one

27. Maritain, *Degrees of Knowledge*, 231.
28. Ibid.   29. Ibid., 232.
30. Ibid.   31. Ibid., 233.

leaves images behind in order to think of Divine Transcendence, it is clear that it demands personality absolutely and necessarily. Personality is the seal of that transcendence."[32] "In Pure Act there is absolute unity, absolute integrity of nature, absolute individuality." Thus, Maritain finds that the notion of "individuality" is one that is predicated analogously. One seeks in Maritain's *Philosophy of Nature*, an analogous predication of the concept "individuation," as it might be said of the organic and inorganic, but he does not broach the topic.[33]

V

Although Maritain never engages in what we today call "textual study," from beginning to end he is through and through a Thomist. He doesn't simply appropriate St. Thomas, he makes the Angelic Doctor's philosophy his own. It is a philosophy used to achieve wisdom within the context of the Faith but used extensively in Maritain's never-ending war on what he takes to be erroneous views of nature and cognition, views that would deprive us of a metaphysics which opens one to the transcendent. From *Antimoderne* to *Le Paysan* Maritain's philosophy is of a single piece. In the abstract his enemies are primarily nominalism, rationalism, positivism, mechanism, and mathematicism. He is to be found correcting Descartes, Kant, Eddington, Russell, Meyerson, Husserl, and scores of contemporaries. He not only draws heavily on the classic commentators of St. Thomas and authors previously mentioned, but he has read Bañez, Gredt, Hoenen, Chenu, Gardeil, Blondel, and Maréchal, among others, sometimes respectfully disagreeing with their interpretation of Aquinas. Gilson and Garrigou-Lagrange may be considered his foremost tutors.

32. Ibid., 234.
33. Jacques Maritain, *La Philosophie de la nature*, trans. Imelda C. Byrne, *Philosophy of Nature* (New York: The Philosophical Library, 1951).

Maritain's Thomism is never without textual foundation, but it is a Thomism that speaks with a twentieth-century accent. In drawing upon St. Thomas's doctrine of "subsistence" and "individuation" Maritain is faithful to the texts, but he employs those notions in a way which Thomas himself never envisaged. This is characteristic of the whole of Maritain's work. It doesn't advance textual study, but it does further the development of a Thomism relevant to the matters we have been discussing. With respect to these key doctrines, it is obvious that one has to interpret St. Thomas in the context of his *Opera omnia*. There are no essay-length, let alone book-length, studies to be found in Aquinas on the problem of individuation. Maritain's interpretation of St. Thomas is certainly a valid reading and is supported in studies by Joseph Owens, Armand Mauer, and Charles A. Hart, to name but a few.[34]

We began with Plato and must end there. The problem of individuation in the sense in which we have been studying it does not arise in most contemporary philosophy. The problem occurs only when a philosopher maintains that there are individuals with natures or essences common to other members of the species. Individuality has to be explained in the presence of commonness.

My reading of contemporary philosophical literature, particularly that of the past decade, suggests that the philosophy of science has taken a realist turn. Various forms of empiricism have failed to account for the success of inference in modern physics and biochemistry, as that which in one generation was postulated as a

---

34. Cf. Joseph Owens, "Thomas Aquinas," in *Individuation in Scholasticism and the Later Middle Ages,* ed. Jorge Gracia (Albany: State University of New York Press, 1994), 173; also "Judgment and Truth in Aquinas," *Medieval Studies* 32 (1970), 138–58; Armand Mauer, *Introduction to Thomas Aquinas: The Division and Methods of the Sciences,* (Toronto: Pontifical Institute of Medieval Studies, 1963), ix–xl. Charles A. Hart, *Thomistic Metaphysics* (Englewood Cliffs, N.J.: Prentice Hall, 1959).

plausible mechanism for observed phenomena has become directly or indirectly visible in another. Realistic interpretations of natural science confront the philosopher with the same problems which begged Aristotle's analysis and Thomas's development thereof. Maritain in confronting the inadequacy of much twentieth-century empiricism was in many respects prescient; he has much to teach *ad mentum divi Thomae*. Through him Aquinas becomes very much a contemporary philosopher.

MARITAIN ON THE LIMITS OF
THE EMPIRIOMETRIC

At the end of the nineteenth century, the European philosophical turf was shared by two main camps, both coalitions: those of an idealistic strain, largely Hegelians, on one side, and the materialists and skeptics, indebted to British empiricism and the *Critiques* of Kant, on the other. The situation was perilous from the vantage point of those who held allegiance to classical antiquity and the religious outlook which had shaped Western culture.

In 1879 Leo XIII recommended in *Aeternae patris* a return to St. Thomas as an antidote to the various materialisms and positivisms which cut one off from the Faith. Maritain in his own right, before he discovered St. Thomas, confronted the vacuity of contemporary systems. He was first attracted to the philosophy of Henri Bergson, but Bergson failed to give him the being-oriented philosophy for which he intuitively longed.[1] Maritain was already an Aristotelian before he began a serious reading of St. Thomas about 1906 under

1. Maritain says of his early mentor, "Bergson sought to overcome the false cult of scientific experience, the mechanistic and deterministic experimentalism which a philosophy of vulgar simplification claimed to be necessary for modern science, yet in Maritain's judgment Bergson's metaphysics remained linked to and dependent upon the science of phenomena, never achieving metaphysics in the Aristotelian sense of the term (Jacques Maritain, *Redeeming the Time* (London: Geoffrey Bles, 1943), 47).

the influence of Ernest Psichari. He was to say later that he was already a Thomist before he had read a word of St. Thomas. That same year he was received into the Church in the company of his Jewish wife Raïssa Oumansoff.

Maritain was not alone in the search for a way out of the prevailing philosophical climate. In reaction to German idealism, which itself was framed as a reaction to Kant's *Critiques,* new and critical realisms were already beginning to emerge on both sides of the Atlantic. Hegel, initially embraced as an antidote to empiricism, was abandoned when it became clear that Hegelians were hard pressed to account for the march of new scientific techniques which were leading to remarkable discoveries in the natural sciences. Above all, Maritain was confronted with August Comte's positivism. Grounded in the British empiricism of the day, Comte not only ruled out metaphysics but ruled out theoretical physics as well for the same reason: a denial of the efficacy of causal reasoning. According to Comte, physics errs as does metaphysics when it postulates abstract entities as explanatory causes. The success of nineteenth- and twentieth-century theoretical physics had yet to undermine positivism as a philosophy of science. Quite apart from its speculative implication, Comte recognized the social implications of the empiricism emanating from the British Isles, implications which led directly to a secular humanism which he codified in his "religion of humanity."

Generally accorded the title, "Father of Positivism," Comte is also regarded as one of the progenitors of sociology. Although Comte's interests led him away from the philosophy of science per se and into the field of sociology, the term he coined came to be used in the wider sense of a philosophy of knowledge which limited knowledge to sensory experience. Hence Maritain's attempt to counter the "brutal empiricism and nominalist pseudo-rationalism" by showing that knowledge is not limited to the descriptive sciences, that ancient truths about nature, human nature, and cognitive ability remain viable and, indeed, vital to humanity. Maritain is later to press the point in a work published under the title, *Redeeming the Time* (sometimes translated as *Ransoming the Time*).[2]

Reflections on the nature and capacity of human knowledge date to the pre-Socratics. Plato's discussion of science and the claims to knowledge by the Greeks, as Maritain recognized, will forever remain a starting point for the philosophy of science. It was Plato who bequeathed to Western philosophy the insight that all science is of the universal. Aristotle concurred, but he found the universal not in some realm of archetypes but in the nature common to members of the species. Aristotle taught that by a process of abstraction we come to know the essence, quiddity, or nature of a thing, prescinding from its accidental features which it may or may not have while remaining the thing that it is. Such is the object of science, the nature of an entity, the structure of a process, their properties and potentialities. Yet to have scientific knowledge is not simply to know what is, not simply to have uncovered a law of nature. For Aristotle to have scientific knowledge is to know the entity, process, or property in the light of its cause or causes. Presupposed by Aristotle are two principles, the principle of causality and the principle of substance, both principles rejected by the British empiricists.

The positivism which Maritain confronted denies at once the intelligibility of nature and the power of intellect to grasp "the more" that is given in the sense report. Maritain offers an elaborate defense of the first principles of thought and being in his *Existence and the Existent,* affirming that there is more in the sense report than the senses themselves are formally able to appreciate.[3] John

2. Maritain, *Redeeming.*
3. Jacques Maritain, *Court traité l'existence et de l'existent,* trans. L. Galantière and G. Phelan, *Existence and the Existent* (New York: Pantheon, 1948).

Locke, in denying the reality of substance, reduces what we call substances to a "constellations of events" or sense reports. According to Locke, we use terms which imply substances, but this usage is merely a shorthand way of pointing to something without repeating at length the properties we associate with that something or constellation. Ockham revisited.

David Hume's account of causality similarly limits knowledge to a simple sense report. We experience succession, Hume tells us, not causality. "Cause" is the name we give to the antecedent, contiguous in place, continuous in time, and habitually associated with the consequent which we designate "effect."

If there are no natures or substances independent of the mind's creating them, if there is no causality, the enterprise of metaphysics collapses. For after all, metaphysics is based on the assumption that the realm of being is greater or wider in designation than the being reported by the senses. If the material order reported by the senses is all there is, then the most general science of reality is natural philosophy or the philosophy of nature. If there is an immaterial order of being as well as the material world of sense, then the most general science or reality is the philosophy of being, also known as metaphysics or ontology. One can conclude to or reach the immaterial order only by a process of reasoning. Such reasoning has led mankind through the ages to affirm the existence of God, to posit an immaterial component of human knowing and a spiritual or immaterial soul.

It is to be noted that the same sort of reasoning that leads one to affirm the existence of God also leads one to affirm the existence of the submicroscopic. As Comte himself recognized, causal reasoning is common to both natural theology and theoretical physics. The efficacy of causal reasoning is dramatically seen in those sciences where the postulated entities of one generation become the encountered ones of another. It can be shown that limiting knowledge to the sense report has implications not only for the natural sciences but for law, the social sciences, and theology as well. On a strict positivist account, science, in effect, is reduced to description and prediction, the social sciences are denied their object, "human nature," and of course natural theology is denied its object since there is no way to reason to the existence of God.

Maritain first takes as his task in developing a philosophy of science the defense of the first principles of thought and being. Put simply, things exist apart from a knowing mind (intelligibility); things are what they are (identity); a thing cannot be and not be at the same time and in the same respect (non-contradiction); a thing is either intelligible in terms of itself or in terms of another (efficient causality or sufficient reason); every agent acts on account of a preconceived end, or, put another way, being in act is intelligible (final causality). These principles are so fundamental that there are none prior to them by which they may be demonstrated. They are the principles upon which all demonstration depends, principles which though they cannot be demonstrated can be defended. Maritain's entire philosophy of science may be regarded as their defense against Locke, Hume, and certain misleading misinterpretations of relativity theory and quantum mechanics.

Maritain next focuses his attention on the abstracting intellect and the degrees of abstraction which make possible the various sciences from physics to metaphysics. In these discussions he displays his indebtedness to Aristotle and Aquinas as well as to the Thomistic interpreters, Cajetan and John of St. Thomas.

Quite apart from his subscription to an Aristotelian-Thomistic theory of knowledge, Maritain was aware that the British empiricists as well as Comte failed to pay much attention to actual practice in the sciences. Maritain begins a chapter of a major work, *The Degrees of Knowledge,* entitled "Philosophy and Experimental Science," by quoting Émile Meyerson, "True science, the only one that we know, is in no way, and in none of its parts in accordance with the positivist scheme."[4] The empiricists notwithstanding, reasoning on a causal basis from the observed to the unobserved is in common practice in the natural sciences. The existence of bacteria was inferred long before the microscope displayed their reality. In physics and chemistry molecular structures were similarly inferred long before electron microscopes and particle accelerators graphically confirmed their reality. It is not misleading to say that in physics causal explanation is taken for granted. The encountered is routinely explained by the non-encountered. No one who looks at the course of nineteenth- and twentieth-century theoretical physics can affirm that science is simply description and prediction.

Maritain had not only studied biology in Heidelberg but was aware of the work of Max Planck, Albert Einstein, Louis de Broglie, Schrödinger, and Werner Heisenberg, to name only a few. He attached particular importance to quantum mechanics and relativity theory because they call into question the validity of certain common-sense conceptions of space and time.

Scientific knowledge, Maritain writes, is knowledge in which, under the compulsion of evidence, the mind points out the reasons why things are the way they are and not otherwise.[5] Science deals with things, but not the flux of the singular. It lays hold of what things are by means of a process of abstraction, discovering their intelligible nature—a universal nature, not the contingent of the singular. "These contingencies of the singular escape science. The necessities of the universal are the proper objects of its grasp."[6] He continues, "The *universality* of the object of knowledge is the

4. Jacques Maritain, "Philosophy and Experimental Science," *Les Degrés du savoir*, trans. G. B. Phelan from the fourth French edition, *The Degrees of Knowledge* (New York: Scribner's, 1959), 21. The English-language translation employed is the one cited here.

5. Ibid., 23.   6. Ibid., 27.

condition of its necessity, the very condition of perfect knowledge or science."[7] The sciences of explanation "set before the mind intelligibles freed from the concrete existence that cloaks them . . . essences delivered from existence in time."[8]

Maritain can quote Aristotle and Aquinas in support of his position. This is the first stage of his attempt to show that metaphysics, indeed science, is possible by pointing to the mind's ability to abstract from the singular to capture the universal or intelligible common nature of many, to see the many as a class. This abstractive power enables us to identify "laws of nature" and is the basis of all taxonomy. Maritain, again following Thomas, calls this the first degree of abstraction. The second degree is mathematical abstraction, the kind of abstraction involved when the mind not only leaves behind the singular, but also the defining characteristics of a class to focus only on the entity as a unit or as something possessing extension or a certain configuration. Thus, arithmetic and geometry and their derivative sciences come into being. We can speak of "five" or "six," leaving behind the fact that we may be talking about bells, books, or candles. Similarly we can talk about the properties of circles, spheres, cones, and straight lines even though none exist as such in reality. Obviously there are circular, spherical, and conical objects in reality, but none is a perfect exemplar of the idealized abstraction.

Maritain discusses at length the so-called intermediate sciences, the physico-mathematical sciences. "Physico-mathematical science," he writes, "is not formally a physical science. Although it is physical as regards the matter in which it verifies its judgments, and although it is oriented toward physical reality and physical causes as the terminus of its investigation, physico-mathematical

7. Ibid.
8. Ibid., 33.

science does not, however, aim to grasp the inner ontological nature itself."[9] Beware of abstractions, he cautions.

Discussing the nature of quantity, extension, and number, he notes that, "the enormous progress made by modern mathematics has rendered more indispensable than ever before the philosophical study of the first principles of mathematical science, which alone can provide a rational account of the true nature of mathematical abstraction and the mental objects which it considers, the properties and mutual relationships of the continuous and discontinuous, the real meaning of *surds* and *transfinite numbers,* the infinitesimal, *non-Euclidian space,* etc. and finally the validity of mathematical transcripts of physical reality, and of such hypotheses, for example, as the theory of relativity."[10]

It is at the third degree of abstraction that the object of metaphysics is attained. At that level the intellect prescinds from every feature, physical and quantitative, to focus on what the whole of reality has in common, namely, being. At this level "the mind can consider objects abstracted from and purified of *all* matter. In this case it considers in things only their very being with which they are saturated, being as such and its laws. These are objects of thought which not only can be *conceived* without matter, but which can even exist without it."[11]

Returning to his discussion of natural science, there are two possible ways, he says, of interpreting the conceptions of modern physics. "The one transports them literally, just as they are, on to the philosophical plane, and thereby throws the mind into a zone of metaphysical confusion. The other discerns their spirit and their noetic value, in an effort to determine their proper import."[12]

One may ask, is real space Euclidean or non-Euclidean? Is the

9. Ibid., 61.
11. Ibid., 36.
10. Ibid., 164.
12. Ibid., 171.

space postulated by the Einsteinian theory of gravitation real or not? The student of modern physics, Maritain responds, must beware of equivocations. The word "real" has not the same meaning for the philosopher, for the mathematician and for the physicist. For the mathematician, a space is "real" when it is capable of mathematical existence, that is to say, when it implies no internal contradiction and duly corresponds to the mathematical notion of space, that is, duly constitutes a system of objects of thought verifying the axioms of geometry.[13]

For the physicist, space is real when the geometry to which it corresponds permits the construction of a physico-mathematical universe in which all our pointer-readings are "explained" and which at the same time symbolizes physical phenomena in a coherent and complete fashion. For a long time Euclidean space sufficed for the interpretations of physics, but today to interpret the measurements it gathers from nature within which geometry and physics are as far as possible amalgamated, it is necessary to have recourse to spherical and elliptical spaces. For us, it is a question of knowing what is real space in the philosophical sense of the word, that is, what is "real" as opposed to an "entity of reason."

Euclidean, Riemannian, and other geometrical entities are "translatable" from one system to another, and all these geometries are equally "true," but they cannot be equally real in the philosophical sense of the word. Mathematical intelligibility by itself alone tells us nothing. The straight line of an elliptical plane and the figure which corresponds to it in a Euclidean model are not different expressions of the same thing. "They are intrinsically different entities belonging to intrinsically different worlds, and from one of these worlds to the other they correspond analogically. To affirm the reality of one space is not to affirm at the same time the reality

13. Ibid., 165–67.

of all the others, but their unreality."[14] Nor will the verification of our senses and of our measuring instruments tell us anything about their reality since with them we quit the mathematical order for the physical order. The mathematical model may serve as a "nucleus of condensation," a model which enables us to correct and interpret the ensemble of measurements taken.

Euclidean space is directly constructible in intuition. Others of necessity are referable to the Euclidean notion of space for their intelligibility. All attempts that have been made to obtain an intuitive representation of non-Euclidean geometries, by Einstein for example, show that these geometries can be rendered imaginable only by reduction to Euclidean geometry. "The model of the thermic universe invented by Poincaré, in which we would be born with the geometry of Lobatchevsky, and that sequence of very simplified sensations that Jean Nicod has thought up and which would give a fictitious subject the idea of the most diverse geometries, confirm by a sort of counter-proof this privilege of Euclidean space."[15] In sum, non-Euclidean geometries presuppose notions of Euclidean geometry. They offer analogical concepts with Euclidean concepts providing the primary analogate. In spite of the use that astronomy makes of them, non-Euclidean space is a being of reason. "It is Euclidean space which appears to the philosopher to be an *ens geometricum reale*."[16] This real geometric space is finite, that is to say, actually existing space is coextensive with the amplitude of the world. Infinite geometric space is a being of reason.

Speaking of the atom presented by the "new physics," Maritain says that physicists tend to form a pure abstract mathematical equivalent of a given atomic structure, which thereby becomes unrepresentable to the imagination and at the same time becomes di-

14. Ibid., 167.   15. Ibid., 168.
16. Ibid., 169.

vested of any ontological meaning. "This equivalent tends to become a more and more fictitious and more and more perfect symbol of the real nature, unknown in itself, of that existing something as other to which determinatively corresponds the name atom. Thus, it knows this nature more and more profoundly, yet more and more enigmatically, and metaphorically, to put it bluntly, in the measure that it constructs the myth—a being in reason founded in *re*—which takes its place."[17]

Maritain then turns to the epistemological conditions and characteristics of a philosophy of nature which undergirds empiriological knowledge in general. He quotes Sir Arthur Eddington who writes that the physicist of today knows "that our knowledge of objects treated in physics consists solely in readings of pointer and other indicators and who knows likewise that 'these pointer readings' are attached to some unknown background."[18]

Like Eddington, Maritain is insistent that a mathematical reading of sensible phenomena cannot speak the last word about the physical real. Physico-mathematical knowledge is not to be mistaken for an undergirding philosophical account of nature. We cannot ask a physico-mathematical approach to give an ontological explanation of the sensible real, let alone an account of human thought and volition. True, the human mind inevitably tends toward a mechanistic philosophy and endeavors to explain everything in terms of extension and movement. "It was bound inevitably," Maritain writes, "to endeavor to make ontological reality intelligible in terms of extension and movement."[19] A Cartesian legacy resurfacing, Maritain might say.

Given that the natural sciences aim at giving a mathematical in-

17. Ibid., 173.

18. Ibid., 173–74.

19. Jacques Maritain, *La Philosophie de la nature,* trans. Imelda C. Byrne, *Philosophy of Nature* (New York: Philosophical Library, 1951), 42.

terpretation of sensible nature, it is easy to conclude, as do many of our contemporaries, that science is capable of explaining the whole ontological reality by extension and movement. But it has yet to do so! "Well, if science cannot do so right away, it will be able later on," is a common refrain when asked for the evidence. The spiritual dimension of man remains elusive, yet the twenty-first century disciples of Hume remain confident that the genome project will eventually disclose all.

Maritain's life work can be read as a rebuttal of contemporary claims that complex organic forms and the spiritual component of human nature are the result of material forces combining with random mutations, the result of necessity and chance, with no creative intelligence behind them. Cultural shifts, if not an outright hedonism, obviously flow from this line of reasoning.

To follow Maritain's every line of argument would require a volume in itself. Throughout his long career and extensive publication he has defended a realism which is not satisfied with a purely empirical or phenomenal account of what is. In the latter half of the twentieth century that realism has gained notable adherents. To mention only two: William A. Wallace, principally in his *The Modeling of Nature*,[20] has carried the Aristotelian-Thomistic analysis into yet another generation; and Rom Harré, in the *Principles of Scientific Explanation*, has shown the necessity of recognizing a nature or structure beyond the empirically given, one that is responsible for measurable traits and is conceptually present to the mind by means of an iconic or sentential model.[21] While Harré remains a materialist, he is not satisfied with the reduction of science to de-

20. William A. Wallace, *The Modeling of Nature: Philosophy of Science and Philosophy of Nature in Synthesis* (Washington, D.C.: The Catholic University of America Press, 1996).

21. Rom Harré, *Principles of Scientific Explanation* (Chicago: University of Chicago Press, 1970).

scription and prediction, which he believes fails to recognize its explanatory character. Others outside the Aristotelian tradition have come to a similar conclusion regarding the nature of scientific inquiry. Yet the recognition of an immaterial order, attainable through reasoned inquiry is far from accepted in today's academic climate and, for the reasons Maritain gives, the failure to acknowledge, put simply, that more is given in the sense report of reality than the senses are able to appreciate.

MARITAIN ON CREATIVE INTUITION
IN ART AND POETRY

I

That attitudes toward science and technology make a difference is widely recognized. If science is conceived as merely description and prediction and not as a search for causes and principles, it will surely be regarded as lacking in explanatory power. Adopting such a positivistic view of science, one automatically rules out certain time-honored disciplines simply because they do not fit the mold. Does something equally momentous flow from varying conceptions of art?

Given the ambiguities found in contemporary usage that not all who use the term "philosophy of art" mean by it the same thing, one can nevertheless identify certain basic questions addressed by those who take up the discipline: What is the end of artistic production? Is or should art be a disinterested endeavor, serving no end beyond itself? What is the relation of art to beauty? To nature? Is art of its essence social? Are certain freedoms to be accorded to the artist which would normally be denied to others? Does artistic production raise a special set of epistemological problems? How describe the artistic process itself?

Maritain, over the period of a career extending from *Art and*

Scholasticism to *Creative Intuition in Art and Poetry,* addresses all of these questions.[1] So, too, in this century, have thinkers as diverse as Leo Tolstoy, John Dewey, and Ortega y Gasset.[2] Recognizing the ambiguity of the discipline and the disparity of effort by those who practice it, it is the purpose of this inquiry, first, to address certain issues which arise in a twentieth-century context and, secondly, to allow Maritain to address those issues as he unfolds his theory of art. The question of social function is quickly addressed; attention is then given to three representative themes of Maritain's outlook: 1) art as a virtue of the practical intellect, 2) the roots of the creative act in the preconscious life of the intellect, and 3) the inescapable role of intellect in artistic production. In addressing these themes, it will become evident that the question of social utility in appraising the fine arts is ill placed.

A philosopher's attitude toward art is of necessity deeply influenced by this theory of knowledge, and it can tell us almost as much about the philosopher as a well-wrought intellectual biography. To use an example from twentieth-century American philosophy, John Dewey's reduction of science to a kind of art form or to technology is a consequence of a long philosophical journey which led him from a youthful Hegelianism to the naturalism of *Experience and Nature* and *Art as Experience.*[3] In Dewey's analysis, art exists not for its own sake but as a problem-solving technique. As

1. Jacques Maritain, *Art and Scholasticism,* trans. J. F. Scanlan (New York: Sheed and Ward, 1930); *Creative Intuition in Art and Poetry* (The A. W. Mellon Lectures) (New York: Pantheon, 1953).

2. Cf. Leo N. Tolstoy, *What is Art?* Trans. A. Marede (New York: Bobbs Merrill, 1960); John Dewey, *Experience and Nature* (New York: Macmillan, 1948); *Art as Experience* (New York: Minton Balch and Co., 1934); José Ortega y Gasset, *The Dehumanization of Art* (Princeton: Princeton University Press, 1968).

3. Dewey's theory of art is contained within his philosophy of science and is regarded by some as the key to his entire philosophy since he reduced science to art or technique.

technique, it has a large and important function in society. Citing Auguste Comte, Dewey refers frequently to the role of art in promoting social goals; he speaks of the moral office and human function of art. As he reads cultural history, the first stirrings of dissatisfaction and the first intimations of a better future are always found in the works of art. Art is the incomparable organ of instruction, the paradigm of knowledge, perfectly combing knowing and doing. Science itself is best understood as art. Like Karl Marx, Dewey subordinates art to the collective. Just as the ultimate criteria of science is its utility, so, too, art is ultimately to be judged by the role it plays in society.

Sometimes the instruction is oblique. Consulting the writings of certain artists themselves, we find the painters Kandinsky and Mondrian, deliberately and for ideological reasons, setting out to destroy natural forms, traditional symbolism, and what they called "superficial imagery" in order to liberate the spirit.[4] Their aim was not to paint something different, but to paint something which resembled as little as possible the objects of ordinary experience.

Concerning the end of art, Maritain not only differs with Dewey but, as shall momentarily be shown, with Ortega and Tolstoy as well. All three authors, Dewey, Ortega, and Tolstoy, concentrate on the practical or social aspect of art. There are profound reasons for this. The insistence on the utility of art is the result of a functional interpretation of intelligence. In the words of Ortega, "A man thinks in order to maintain himself among things."[5] Even Maritain's mentor, Henri Bergson, defined man as *homo faber* not *homo sapiens;* man is made to fabricate.[6] Leo Tolstoy links art to

4. For an interesting discussion of modern art see José Ortega y Gasset, *Dehumanization of Art*, 21ff. Cf. Maritain, *Creative Intuition in Art and Poetry*, 215–21. Maritain's sympathetic yet critical reflections are discussed later.

5. Ortega y Gasset, *Dehumanization*, 196.

6. Henri Bergson, *The Two Sources of Religion and Morality* (New York: Holt, 1935).

communication and judges it in terms of its effectiveness in facilitating intercourse between man and man.[7] To define art, says the author of *War and Peace,* we must conceptually divorce it from beauty, or from that which pleases us, and consider it as one of the conditions of human life. Art is the transmission of feelings we have judged to be important. The emphasis is on transmission. By contrast, Maritain devotes an entire chapter to the defense of the principles. Art by itself tends to the good of the works not to the good of the man. The first responsibility of the artist, he insists, is toward his work.[8] Its transcendent end is beauty.

What are we to make of these seemingly contradictory views on the nature of art? It is perhaps a truism to say the "philosophers are not so much wrong in what they affirm as they are in what they deny." A simple distinction, second nature to Maritain, but one apparently neglected by Tolstoy and Ortega, would help set the matter straight. I have in mind the distinction between servile and fine art which acknowledges the instrumental character of much artistic production while leaving the way open for art which serves no other purpose than to please. That which pleases can at the same time communicate. The pleasure it gives may be due in part to the nobility of the subject matter it portrays or to the sentiment it conveys. But if edification or the communication of a message is made paramount, the artifact is apt to fail and to take on the character of a mere instrument.

Maritain can appreciate art for its own sake primarily because he has a classical notion of intellect. As the Greeks respected natural forms and enjoyed their beauty, so too, they respected disinterested inquiry for its own sake. Knowledge does not have to end in making or doing to be worthwhile; knowledge is its own end. Maritain is Greek in this respect. Just as the aim of science is under-

7. Tolstoy, *What is Art?* 49.
8. Maritain, *Art and Scholasticism* (New York: Scribner's, 1960), 38–63.

standing, not power or technology, so, too, the fine arts have as their primary end the disclosure of being under the aspect of beauty. Science may issue in technology, the fine arts themselves may serve, but both exist primarily to satisfy the mind's appetite for knowledge and beauty.

Significantly, in defending the instrumental or practical character of knowledge, John Dewey denies the reality of science understood as a quest for intelligibility in the light of causes and principles. Science for Dewey is description and prediction. Its aim is the manipulation of material in the light of agreed-upon ends. Interesting, too, is the moralism that runs through much of Dewey's philosophy, a moralism that is absent in Maritain although he wrote a book called *The Responsibility of the Artist.* In that book Maritain condemns "art for the social group." What is called *l'art engagé,* enlisted art or drafted art, he believes is inevitably propaganda art, either for moral or anti-moral, social, political, religious, or anti-religious purposes. "Art, like knowledge, is appendant to values which are independent of the interest, even the noblest interests, of human life, for they are the values of the intellectual order."[9] Maritain is neither moralist nor reformer. He is the philosopher utilizing the categories of being in order to understand. His is the legacy of Aristotle and Aquinas.

The essays which first brought him attention were published in French in 1920 under the title *Art et scolastique* (the English translation appeared ten years later in 1930). His continued reflections on art eventually gained for him an invitation to deliver the inaugural series of the Andrew W. Mellon Lectures at the National Gallery of Art in Washington, soon to become the most prestigious series in North America. (Etienne Gilson was later to give the fourth set of lectures in that annual series.)

The Mellon lectures were published as *Creative Intuition in Art*

9. Jacques Maritain, *The Responsibility of the Artist* (New York: Scribner's, 1960).

and Poetry. In them Maritain, using poetry as the primary example, attempts to analyze the preconscious life of the intellect in the creative act. His analysis presupposes an Aristotelian theory of the virtues and a Thomistic epistemology. In the process of employing those instruments in an area he knows well, Maritain succeeded in sharpening his theory of knowledge itself. In *Creative Intuition in Art and Poetry* Maritain recognizes many modern enemies, among them subjectivism, irrationalism, and instrumentalism. He emerges from battle where we might expect him to be, faithful to the classical tradition as represented by Aristotle and Aquinas.

II

To examine some of the principal themes of *Creative Intuition in Art and Poetry* is to discover not only a philosophy of art but an epistemology and a metaphysics. Critics have remarked that the book is not an easy one, and that judgment is to some extent true. But in spite of its philosophical abstruseness there is a certain freshness and elegance to it.

Maritain's fundamental perceptions are derivative. He inherits from Aristotle and the scholastics a theory of knowledge and a theory of the virtues, but Maritain makes this advance. By reflecting primarily on poetry, he is positioned to examine in microscopic detail the intellect as it creates. His choice of poetry as the exemplary form of art is in part attributable to his wife, Raïssa, herself a poet. Within their circle of friends, there were not only poets but painters, sculptors, and musicians of rank. From those friends Maritain was to gain valuable insights into the creative process. His problem was to understand that process as a philosopher.

Two things are required of one who would follow Maritain's analysis of intelligence and the creative process: 1) acquaintance with the Thomistic theory of knowledge, and 2) the experience of having written a poem. For Aquinas, two intellectual powers can be identified: the "abstracting" or "agent intellect," and the "passive" or "understanding intellect." The agent intellect, which Thomas thought is the faculty by which man most resembles God Himself, is a power that is constantly in act. Like a never-ceasing beam of light the agent intellect illuminates objects presented to it by means of the senses. Intellectual knowing is contingent on sense experience but is not reducible to sense experience. The intellect is able to discern in the empirically given data elements which the senses themselves are formally not able to appreciate. That same intellect is not only able to abstract from the singular to the universal but is able to *express* what it knows in an act called "understanding." Before the mind even forms a concept, there is a pre-conscious mingling or merging of sensory with intellectual materials. The vagaries of mingling, grouping, and insight depend upon an individual's intellectual history, the habits acquired over a lifetime. You and I, confronted with the same pastoral landscape, may comprehend in a similar manner but only to a point. What we make of that landscape depends upon previous experience and the habits of learning which each of us has acquired. We are sometimes furious with a friend who "cannot see the woods for the trees," but then we realize that he or she hasn't been prepared to "see." Not everyone is capable of the same degree of abstract thought or even of the same degree of appreciation of natural forms. As conceptual ability varies, so, too, does artistic ability and the ability to appreciate. To avoid racing ahead to Maritain's conclusion, however, it is necessary to allow his argument to unfold as he himself presents it.

The speculative intellect, Maritain maintains, knows only for the sake of knowledge. It longs to "see," and only to "see." Truth, or the grasping of that which is, is its only goal and its only life.[10] The

10. Maritain, *Creative Intuition*, 49.

practical intellect, on the other hand, knows for the sake of action. "From the very start its object is not *being* to be grasped, but human activity to be guided and human tasks to be achieved."[11] Practical intellect is immersed in creativity. "Its very life is to mold intellectually that which will be brought into being, to judge about ends and means, and to direct and even to command our powers of execution."[12]

Two kinds of practical activity must be distinguished. Moral judgment or prudence is to be differentiated from artistic judgment, though both are concerned with means to ends.

The difference between prudence and art is this: prudence is the intellectual determination of actions to be done; art, by contrast is the intellectual determination of works to be made. With respect to works made, a further distinction is to be drawn, namely, that between the useful and the fine arts. The former satisfy a specific need and are governed by the exigencies of that end or need. The fine arts are motivated, on the other hand, not by a particular need but by the demand of the will to release the pure creativity of the spirit in its longing for beauty. The will tends to this end according to rules discovered by the intellect. The end is beauty and not a particular need to be satisfied. In art, as in contemplation, intellectuality goes beyond concepts and discursive reasoning and is achieved through a "congeniality" or "co-naturality" with the object, which love alone can bring about. To produce in beauty, says Maritain, the artist must be in love with beauty.[13]

The distinction between the useful and fine arts is not to be understood in too absolute a manner. The Greeks were aware that in the humblest work the craftsman or the artisan is also properly concerned with beauty. Maritain prefers to distinguish between

11. Ibid.   12. Ibid.
13. Ibid., 58.

the two using the terms "subservient" and "self-sufficient." The fine arts, because of their immediate relation to beauty and to the creativity of the spirit are free; they belong to the world of liberal arts. Intuitive or nondiscursive reasoning will in a large measure determine their character. Nevertheless, the fine arts, from the very fact that they belong in the generic realm of art, participate in the law of useful arts. Thus the conceptual, discursive, logical reason, or better, the working reason, plays a necessary though secondary part in the fine arts. This part is only instrumental because it relates to the particular ways of making an object. If it gets the upper hand, it destroys the work of fine art.[14]

The normal climate of art is intelligence and learning. The intellect is reflective by nature; even the practical virtues cannot develop in their own sphere without a more or less simultaneous development of reflectivity. And the name of reflective intelligence in the domain of art is critical reason. An artist cannot be guided by instinct alone.[15]

How, then, explain certain seemingly irrational tendencies in modern art? In Maritain's judgment modern art endeavors to free itself from nature and the forms of nature. It seeks liberation from the conventions of language and form and is consequently marked by a tendency to be obscure. In twentieth-century art there is a decided movement away from conceptual, logical, and discursive reasoning. Though modern art may at times display a suicidal attitude of contempt for reason, it is by no means, in its essence, a process of liberation from reason itself. Reason possesses a life both deeper and less conscious than its articulate logical life for prior to logical reason there is intuitive reason.[16]

Maritain distinguishes between a conscious and a pre-con-

14. Ibid., 63.   15. Ibid., 65.
16. Ibid., 73ff.

scious life of intellect. The pre-conscious life of the intellect he identifies with the initial activity of the agent intellect, the first stage in the birth of a concept. Part of his break with Bergson was the result of Maritain's conviction that the Thomistic doctrine of agent intellect better allowed him to understand the pre-conscious wellsprings of creativity.

In spite of these distinctions, Maritain is careful to present man as a single entity; man is neither intellect nor body, neither spirit nor sense. The imagination proceeds or flows form the essence of the soul through the intellect; the external senses proceed from the essence of the soul through the imagination for they exist in man to serve the imagination.[17] Concepts and images can belong to the pre-conscious. The common root of all the powers of the soul is the spiritual unconscious. In this root activity, the intellect and the imagination, as well as the powers of desire, love, and emotion, are engaged in common. The powers of the soul envelop one another, the universe of sense perception is in the universe of imagination, which is in the universe of intelligence.[18]

All powers within the intellect are stirred and activated by the light of the illuminating intellect. According to the order of the ends and demands of nature, the imagination and the senses are raised in man to a state genuinely human where they somehow participate in intelligence, and their exercise is, as it were, permeated with intelligence. Thus Maritain can say, "poetry is the fruit neither of the imagination nor of the intellect alone. . . . It proceeds from the totality of man, sense, imagination, intellect, love, desire, instinct, blood, and spirit, together."[19]

Maritain characterized poetic knowledge as "affective," as "knowledge through inclination," as "a co-naturality or congeniality" in which the intellect is at play, not alone, but together with the

17. Ibid., 107.   18. Ibid., 110.
19. Ibid., 111.

affective inclinations and dispositions of the will, and as guided and shaped by them. Poetic knowledge is not rational knowledge, knowledge through the conceptual, logical and discursive exercise of reason, but it is, nevertheless, genuine knowledge, although it is obscure and perhaps incapable of giving an account of itself. Poetic knowledge is born in the unconsciousness of the spirit. It is essentially creative and tends to express itself in a work.[20]

"Poetic intuition is not directed toward essences," says Maritain, "for essences are disengaged from concrete reality in a concept, a universal idea, and scrutinized by means of reasoning."[21] Essences are an object of speculation; they are not the thing grasped by poetic intuition. "Poetic intuition is directed toward concrete existence as conatural to the soul pierced by a given emotion."[22] But poetic intuition does not stop at a given existent, a given particular, but transcends it, in the manner of a sign that stands for something more. Things are not only what they are, they refer beyond themselves, suggesting more than they actually possess. Poetic intuition can neither be learned nor improved by exercise and discipline for it depends on a certain natural function, natural freedom of the soul and the imaginative faculties, and on the natural strength of the intellect. Though poetic activity is by nature subjective, it is still disinterested. It engages the human "self" in its deepest recesses, but in no way for the sake of the ego. Self-revelation is always for the sake of the art work.

Continuing his analysis of poetry, Maritain finds himself in a position to say something about beauty. He accepts Aquinas's analysis which recognizes in the thing called beautiful three essential characteristics: integrity, proportion, and clarity *(splendor formae)*[23] While beauty is a transcendental in the Thomistic sense, and everything which exists, to the extent that it exists, may be

---

20. Ibid., 117–18.
22. Ibid., 126.

21. Ibid., 125–26.
23. Ibid., 160ff.

called beautiful, aesthetic beauty, says Maritain, is the beauty most naturally proportioned to the human mind. Aesthetic beauty may be regarded as a particular determination of transcendental beauty. It is transcendental beauty as confronting not simply the intellect but the intellect and sense activity together. Beauty, Maritain suggests, is not the object but the "end beyond the end" of poetry. In the case of plastic and visual art, the cognitive function of the intellect is entirely subordinated to its creative function. The intellect knows in order to create. Poetry, by contrast, is essentially free. There is nothing that may exercise command or mastery over it. In poetry there is only the urge to give expression to that knowledge which is poetic intuition and in which both the subjectivity of the poet and the realities of the world awake obscurely in a single awakening. In a certain sense, poetry has no object; it creates its own object. Poetry tends toward beauty but not toward beauty as an object to be known or to be made. A better way to put it is to say that poetry, in effecting its proper end, engenders beauty. Like other fine arts it tends more intimately to produce a good work than to produce a beautiful work. The fine arts cannot make beauty their end. To the extent to which they make beauty an object, their object, and in tending toward beauty, forget that beauty is more than an operational end—being the end beyond the end—they recede from beauty. Beauty is achieved almost accidentally as a by-product of the work produced.

III

Maritain utilizes his analysis of poetry in an attempt to give a sympathetic reading to much twentieth-century painting.[24] Nonrepresentative painting, he recognizes, breaks away from nature; it turns away from things and the grasping of things and renounces seeing into the inner depths of nature. In breaking away from the

24. Ibid., 209ff.

existential world of nature, nonrepresentative art condemns itself
to fall short of its own dearest purposes and the very ends for the
sake of which it came into being. Cut off from the poetic grasp of
things, nonrepresentative art will attain only the most limited
form of beauty, namely, the mute beauty of the best balanced objects produced by the mechanical arts. There is no exercise of the
free creativity of the spirit without poetic intuition. The crucial
mistake of abstract art has been—unwittingly—to reject poetic intuition and, therefore, to reject systematically the existential world
of things. All in all, abstract art, taken as a system, is in the same
predicament as idealist philosophy; both are walled in.[25]

As an exercise or experiment, nonrepresentative painting has
value, but primarily as technique. It is Maritain's opinion that nonrepresentative art reflects a period of stagnation or regression
rather than an advancement or progress in the history of art. Its
great mistake has been to put the instrumental and the secondary
before the principal and the primary. Another mistake has been to
conceive of forward movement only in terms of a flight from natural forms. The mistake has been to look for freedom from something, at first from a servile imitation or copying of natural appearances, but eventually from the existential world of nature
itself. Instead of looking for freedom to achieve in one's work a
more and more genuine revelation both of things and the self, it
has denied any referent against which it can be measured. Contemporary painting will get out of its predicament when it understands that the only way to effective transposition, deformation,
recasting, or transfiguration of natural appearances is through the
insight provided by poetic intuition. Poetic intuition does as it
pleases with natural appearances, not by any technical trick, but by
virtue of its inner pressure.[26]

25. Ibid., 220.
26. Ibid., 223–26.

IV

Given its twentieth-century course, it is Maritain's judgment that poetry has never been in greater need of reason, of genuine human wisdom.[27] Wisdom presupposes a realm of knowledge, which pertains to the poet not as a poet but as a man, and on which depends the universe of thought presupposed by his activity as a poet. The allurements of magic must be counterbalanced by the judgmental character of rational knowledge. Poetry may be the heaven of working reason, a divination of the spiritual things of sense. Poetry may be truly spiritual nourishment, but it does not satiate; it only makes a man hungrier. That hunger has to be fed by sources other than poetry, though poetry in a peculiar way is proximate to those sources. In a certain sense, poetry is akin to mystical experience, for both poetic and mystic insight are born near one another in the center of the soul. In another sense, poetry is not unlike metaphysics. "Metaphysics snatches at the spiritual in an idea through the most abstract intellection; poetry reaches it in a flash by the very point of the sense sharpened through intelligence."[28] Poetic knowledge analogically participates in the contemplative character of philosophy for it is knowledge of the very interiority of things. Thus, because in its own way it is spiritual communion with being, poetry transcends those arts which are entirely encompassed in and committed to practical knowledge in the strict sense of the word, knowledge only to make. It is because of this transcendence that poetry enjoys a universal dominion over all the arts which have to do with beauty.

Poetic experience is, for the most part, a transient and fleeting experience. This experience is, to a large extent, hidden in the preconscious. Thus when we look for some verbal expression bearing

27. Ibid., 234.
28. Ibid., 235.

witness to the inner experience of composers and painters, we are often obliged to satisfy ourselves with the external and indirect.[29]

The "poetic sense, in the work, corresponds to the poetic experience in the poet."[30] The poetic sense is to the poem what the soul is to man. "It is the poetic intuition itself communicated to the work in its native, pure and immediate efficacy."[31] It might be said that the poetic sense is the inner melody of the poem. The logical or intelligible sense is only one of the elements or components of the poetic sense. "The poetic sense is an immanent meaning made up of meanings: the intelligible meanings of the words . . . the imaginal meanings of the words . . . the musical relations between the words, and between the meaningful contents with which the words are laden. Thus the intelligible sense, through which the poem utters ideas, is entirely subordinate to the poetic sense."[32] It is with respect to the intelligible sense that a poem is clear or obscure. "A poem may be obscure or it may be clear," says Maritain, "what matters is only the poetic sense."[33] The law of intelligibility imposed by tradition has been the occasion for innumerable mediocre poems, where the logical sense was made to prevail over the poetic sense. But modern poetry, swarming with obscure poems both good and bad, has effected full recognition of the necessary primacy of the poetic sense.

No poem can be completely obscure "for no poem can completely get rid of the intelligible sense."[34] A poem cannot be without poetic sense and intelligible meaning, subordinate though it may be. "Conversely, no poem can be absolutely clear, since no poem can receive its being from the intelligible or sense uniquely."[35] Some poems, it may be noted, are only seemingly obscure; others are obscure in essence.

29. Ibid., 250–51.
30. Ibid., 257.
31. Ibid., 258.
32. Ibid., 259.
33. Ibid.
34. Ibid.
35. Ibid., 261.

The very first effect and sign of poetic knowledge and poetic intuition, as soon as they exist in the soul, "is a kind of musical stir,
and unformulated song, with no words, no sounds, absolutely inaudible to the ear, audible only to the heart."[36] How account for
this fact? On the one hand there is an actual flash of knowing, born
through spiritualized emotion. On the other hand there is "a spiritual milieu—a kind of fluid and moving world, activated by the
diffuse light of the Illuminating Intellect, and seemingly asleep but
secretly tense and vigilant—which is the pre-conscious life of the
intellect, and of imagination and of emotion, empty of any actual
concept or idea, but full of images and full of emotional move-
ments, and in which all the past experiences and treasures of
memory acquired by the soul are present in a state of virtuality. It
is within this fluid and moving milieu that poetic experience and
poetic intuition exist, not virtually, but as an act or actuation defi-
nitely formed."[37]

Maritain continues, "The expansion of the poetic intuition in
its vital milieu develops, and at the same time, the intuitive pulsions also expand and become more and more distinct; explicit
images awaken, more distinct emotions resound in the fundamental emotion. Then there is in the soul of the poet an enlarged musical stir, a music no longer almost imperceptible, but more and
more cogent, in which the soundless rhythmic and harmonic relations between intuitive pulsions, together with their soundless
melody emerge into consciousness. This enlarged musical stirring
is the spontaneous start of operative exercise. With it the process of
expression begins, in a first transient and tendential stage."[38] It
tends to verbal expression. But the actual verbal expression of this
musical stirring constitutes a second and distinct stage. There are,

36. Ibid., 301.
37. Ibid.
38. Ibid., 302–3.

therefore, two distinct musics, two essentially distinct stages in poetic expression: the music of intuitive pulsions within the soul, and the music of words which will pass outside of the soul.

Poetry cannot do without music. The primary role of music in poetry is not the music of words but the internal music of the intuitive pulsions. There has been a reversion of introversion, from an externalization to an internalization of music. Without modern poetry we may never have become fully aware of the importance of this inaudible, wordless and soundless music. It is easy to verify such observations if we read modern poets exercising at the same time our power of introspection and paying attention not only to the words but to what they produce within ourselves. "A poem is an engine to make us pass through or beyond things."[39] The classical poem aims to express and signify the trans-reality caught by creative intuition, but in order to do so, it must use the instrumentality of definite things which stand as objects of thought, and are signified by logically organized concepts. The modern poem signifies only the trans-reality caught by poetic intuition, without being bound first to signify a definite set of things standing as objects of thought. It has, thus, one single significance which has to do with poetic intelligence, not with rationalized and socialized communicability. "The music of words in modern poetry, still necessary as it may be, yields the foremost place to another, more internal music. Music is pushed back inwardly. What matters essentially now is the music of intuitive pulsions, which passes into the work of words freely—without being repressed or obliterated by the exigencies of the logos—and to which the reader in his turn is finally taken by this work of words."[40] Modern poetry, as the immediate expression of this internal music, is thus given intelligibility in terms of its source and attainment.

39. Ibid., 318.
40. Ibid., 321.

Finally, three aspects or levels of poetry—Maritain calls them "Aepipharies of creative intuition"—are identified. The first and most basic intentional value in the poem, he says, is the poetic sense.[41] It is followed by the action and the theme which are complements or objective reflections of the poetic sense. The third may be called "number" or "harmonic expansion." Through the latter the poetic sense and the action are complemented or externally reflected, in the same way, analogically speaking, as natural substances are extended by quantity. The number or harmonic expansion of the poem is the vital concurrence of the multiple, or the vital order, bringing to complex orchestral unity parts struggling to assert their own individual claims. It is through harmonic expansion that the work is possessed of a kind of external music. For the extent to which it has number, its visible or sonorous qualities, its impact on the senses and power of delighting them, its own charge of sensitivity and sensuousness are penetrated with the secret measure of reason and logic. Harmonic expansion becomes the vital order.

Put another way, the three stages of creative intuition may be identified as: first, the pre-conscious, nonconceptual life of the intellect, and this is the state of the poetic sense from which the poem receives its essence; secondly, the state of nascent logos where the work exists as thought and is given its action and theme; and thirdly, the state of formed logos or the work in making in which the poetic intuition passes into the poem through the instrumentality of the number or harmonic expansion. These are the three epiphanies of poetic intuition or creative emotion. Relating this analysis to the three aspects of the beautiful previously noted, Maritain writes: "Radiance or clarity, which is the absolutely primary property of beauty, and matters first of all, appears

41. Ibid., 354–405.

principally (I do not say uniquely) in the poetic sense or inner melody of the work; integrity, in the action and the theme; and consonance, in the number or harmonic Structure."[42]

V

With this account of the creative process behind us, the questions we raised at the beginning of this chapter seem almost naive. Whether or not our personal experience is deep enough to verify every aspect of Maritain's reflections on art and the creative process, he clearly shows that for anyone who would be fully human, artistic production is a necessity. Just as all men are called to a life of contemplation so all are called to a life of creativity, a creativity that has no end other than the delight it produces.

This is not to say that fine art cannot serve. Art in the service of the temple is a case in point, but Maritain's genius is this: he has graphically shown how intimately associated with human nature is the disposition to create. To be fully human is to bring into being works which stand apart from the self, but which nevertheless reflect the innermost aspects of the artists's being. That revelatory act is not self-centered or subjective but is instead directed toward disclosing the real which is the object of both artist and viewer. The vocation of an artist is an aspect of the human vocation, namely, self-perfection. Not all who attempt to create will emerge among the ranks of the immortals, but all are called.

Gabriel Marcel once remarked that the spirit of our age is basically "ontophobic." Maritain by contrast consciously grounds his theory of art in a metaphysics of nature and human nature and in doing so achieves a certain power which others such as Dewey do not possess. Maritain is open to a transcendent dimension of experience, both little "t" and big "T." He is open to the perennial or the

42. Ibid., 370.

time-transcendent, and to Transcendent Being Itself. Because Maritain understands the relevance of the past, appreciating the role of the inherited, he better understands making. He is also in a position to judge outcomes. By a law of human nature, the now-directed is incapable of evaluating even the now.

On this point Ortega and Maritain would be in complete agreement. Ortega writes, "Only in proportion as we are desirous of living more do we really live. . . . Obstinately to insist on carrying on within the same familiar horizon betrays weakness and a decline in vital energies." But "To excel the past we must not allow ourselves to lose contact with it; on the contrary, we must feel it under our feet because we have raised ourselves upon it." How different is the outlook of Dewey, for whom "custom," "habit," and the "inherited" veil the eye's ability to perceive. For the now-directed Dewey, the only problem is the mechanical one at hand. For Maritain, artistic production reflects a time-transcending intellectual awareness, an awareness grounded not only in the immediate but also in the experience of previous generations as disclosed through history, but above all in insights gleaned from theology and philosophy.

The artist is not simply a technician; for in creating, the artist discloses the possibilities of being. He is not, as Tolstoy would make him, merely a communicator of his own subjective feeling. The artist more than any other human being participates in the divine creative act, bringing into being an object which at once satisfies intellect under the aspect of "truth," the will under the aspect of "good," and the whole man under the aspect of "beauty." To my knowledge, no one has rendered more attractive the high vocation of artist than Maritain. One puts down *Creative Intuition in Art and Poetry* wondering if the book, in fact, is not one love song to his wife Raïssa.

VII

JOHN RAWLS AND JACQUES MARITAIN

ON THE *LAW OF PEOPLES*

In a commencement address delivered at the University of Notre Dame in May 2000, United Nations Secretary-General Kofi Annan said, "It is particularly shameful that the United States, the most prosperous and successful country in the history of the world, should be one of the least generous in terms of the share of its gross national product it devotes to helping the world's poor."[1] He admitted that the United States is the second highest contributor in foreign aid after Japan in absolute terms, spending close to $9 billion a year, but he called for debt relief and for volunteers to train groups of people in poor nations in the use of information technology. Kofi Annan offered no description, let alone justification, of principles that would require such a financial commitment on the part of the United States. Seemingly, justice, not charity, demands it. Kofi Annan cited John Paul II's "burning desire to see the benefits of human progress more widely and equitably shared," concurring with him in the hope that given the world's increasing interdependence, individuals and peoples will accept "responsibility for their fellow human beings, for all the earth's inhabitants."

1. Reuters, May 22, 2000.

John Paul II has frequently urged rich nations to assist poor ones. His appeal is made both within a theological context and within the natural-law tradition and its concept of the brotherhood of mankind. John Paul II prefers the term "human solidarity."

In the largely secular world of the West, distinctively Christian morality has lost some of its efficacy as a motivator. But certain principles remain difficult to ignore or repudiate. Since the Enlightenment, philosophers have attempted to justify, on purely secular grounds, principles grounded in Christianity. This is reflected in the plethora of metaphors suggesting responsibilities heretofore unacknowledged. We speak of a "global village" and the responsibility of the "international community" to "underdeveloped countries." John Paul II himself speaks of the "rich North" and "impoverished South." A cosmopolitan outlook is thought to trump national concerns. No program, national or international, is proposed without moral justification. Often that justification is advanced without any reference to a supporting concept of nature and human nature and often in contravention to the otherwise purely materialistic philosophy of the proponent. Echoing Hobbes and Rousseau, John Dewey, for example, assumed it to be one of his tasks to provide a pragmatic or naturalistic justification of those values formerly supported on "supernaturalistic" grounds, grounds critical intelligence can no longer accept.

One of the most recent attempts in the tradition of Dewey to justify global concerns is that of John Rawls. The parameters of discourse have shifted somewhat. Dewey had to contend only with Western modes of thought, working within an inherited Western culture, in which traditional morality was more or less intact. Rawls has to contend with "multiculturalism" and "procedural democracy," the latter barring governing authorities from favoring any one concept of the good. Dewey's task was to defend traditional morality on purely materialistic grounds. Now with that morality having virtually disappeared, Rawls has had to start from scratch, so to speak. One can appreciate the enormity of his task, deprived of the natural law tradition and unable to acknowledge the biblical roots of Western culture.

In reading John Rawls's, the *Law of Peoples*[2] and Christopher Morris's *An Essay on the Modern State*,[3] I noted with some interest that the issues these authors consider were addressed by Jacques Maritain in the Walgreen Lectures that he delivered at the University of Chicago in 1949 and published as *Man and the State*.[4] On the surface the pragmatic naturalistic approach of Rawls would seem to be the antithesis of the natural-law approach of Maritain, although in the last analysis Rawls comes close to a natural-law justification of his distributionist policies. Morris, like Maritain, challenges the notion that nations are sovereign entities.

Rawls is perhaps the best known and most often quoted contemporary philosopher in North America. No graduate student of philosophy in any Western university is unaware of his seminal work, *A Theory of Justice* (1971). The James B. Conant Professor Emeritus of Harvard University has in the *Law of Peoples* expanded his theory of justice from that of a single, liberal, democratic society to "the global network of nations," extending the idea of justice as fairness developed in *A Theory of Justice* to "the society of peoples." Within the context of modern constitutional democracy, Rawls strives for principles which may underlie political consensus among citizens of different political, religious, and philosophical outlooks. On what can citizens of different ideological commitments agree? This is not a question easily answered by Rawls as he

2. John Rawls, *Law of Peoples* (Cambridge: Harvard University Press, 1999).

3. Christopher Morris, *An Essay on the Modern State* (Cambridge: Cambridge University Press, 1998).

4. Jacques Maritain, *Man and the State* (Chicago: University of Chicago Press, 1950).

seeks to construct principles of justice which permit men of rival moral traditions to co-exist in peace. Given Rawls's basic philosophical commitments, his comprehensive theory of justice must be construed without reference to any one conception of the good. Moral diversity and competing claims with respect to the good are taken as a basic fact.

Recognizing that a liberal society requires virtuous conduct on the part of its citizens, Rawls identifies those basic virtues as "political cooperation," "a sense of fairness," "tolerance," and "a willingness to meet others half way." Yet it is obvious that for Rawls justice is not just a moral virtue to be acquired but a political program to be achieved. In extending the idea of a social contract to the "society of peoples," Rawls is admittedly indebted to the liberal conception of justice grounded in Locke, Rousseau, and Kant and to Mill's utilitarianism. The law of peoples that Rawls envisions is explicitly an extension of the liberal conception of justice grounded in Locke, Rousseau, and Kant. His aim is to articulate a set of universally acceptable principles applicable to the regulation of mutual political relations between peoples. The conditions under which this might be attained are constitutional liberties, i.e., religious freedom, liberty of conscience, political freedom, and equal justice for women.

Rawls counts on those who hold different and irreconcilable comprehensive doctrines to be of common mind in supporting the idea of equal liberty for all. Wary of according religion the role of moral tutor, he invokes the partisan doctrine of separation of church and state, relegating religion to the purely private sphere.

In *Man and the State,* Maritain recognizes that men possessing quite different, even opposite, metaphysical and religious outlooks can reach a *modus vivendi.* We may recognize, writes Maritain, a distinction between a practical creed which lies at the root of common life and the theoretical justification of such proffered by different philosophical and religious systems. The body politic has the right and duty to promote this practical creed among its citizens, mainly through education, for on it depends national communion and civil peace. To continue with Maritain, the state has no right to impose on its citizens or to demand from them a rule of faith or conformity of reason, or impose a philosophical or religious creed which would present itself as the only possible justification of the practical charter. Rawls would agree that the philosophical and religious creeds are important, although he would make them a purely private affair.

Rawls's society of peoples depends on a common reverence for truth and intelligence, human dignity, freedom, brotherly love, and the value of moral good, but the wellsprings of this reverence are not addressed. If Rawls has a major oversight, it is his failure to explore the roots of a Western culture he seems to take for granted. A society that does not recognize and promote the public culture on which it is grounded is not likely to foster the social stability which Rawls deems a condition for his "realistic utopia" (his words). Social stability cannot be merely a *modus vivendi* but must be rooted in a shared conception of rights and justice. Acknowledging that religious, philosophical, and moral unity are not possible, Rawls discounts their necessity provided a reasonable idea of toleration prevails. Of course when nothing is prized, as in Rawls' procedural democracy, everything can be tolerated. It may be easier to make the case that tolerance is a vice than to justify its putative status as a virtue. No society can tolerate disrespect for its laws; no state, anarchy. Any institution must preserve its unity to preserve its very existence. Until recently this was understood as a basic principle of good government, be it in the intellectual, moral, ecclesiastical, or political realm. Roget's English Language *Dictionary of Synonyms and Antonyms* under "tolerance" gives as synonyms leniency, clemency, indulgence, laxity, sufferance, concession, and permissiveness, terms generally regarded as designating questionable behavior. Of course, certain technical meanings of the term may be identified. "Tolerance" in biology, for example, is the ability of an organism to endure contact with a substance or its introduction into the body without ill effects. "Tolerance" in the industrial order is the range within which a dimension of a machine part may vary. "Religious tolerance," which Rawls principally has in mind, is the intellectual and practical acknowledgment of the right of others to live in accord with religious beliefs not accepted as one's own.

Discounting the role of religion in society, Rawls envisages a thoroughly secular state. His commonwealth is solely concerned with the material well being of its citizens. Spiritual well being is the burden of the individual. Ignored is the role which religion has played in the West, indeed in creating the great civilizations of the world. No philosophical system has yet surpassed religion as a moral tutor. In fact, Western man, in spite of contemporary trends, has no experience of living in a purely secular society.

Turning now to Maritain's reflections on the possibility of global unity, Maritain is convinced that the interdependence of nations is essentially an economic interdependence, not something politically agreed upon, willed and built up.[5] It has come to be by virtue of a merely technical or material process, not by virtue of a simultaneous political or rational process.

Economic interdependence alone, Maritain continues, is not likely to produce international accord, given the rival needs and prides of nations. The question our civilization is facing now is whether human conscience and moral intelligence will be able to direct technological achievement to the service of mankind as a whole, countering man's instinctive greed. Unfortunately, we live

5. Ibid., 189.

in a world more and more economically one and more and more divided by the pathological claims of opposed nationalisms.

Paul VI claimed Maritain as his teacher; John Paul II may well be a second-generation student. Speaking on the occasion of the reception of the new Greek Ambassador to Vatican City,[6] John Paul II noted: "Diplomacy must face the challenges presented by globalization." Only in this way will it be possible "to overcome threats to peace and development, such as the poverty of countless human beings, social inequalities, ethnic tensions, environmental pollution, and respect for human rights and political freedom." John Paul II emphasized that in order to avoid anarchy, this globalized world needs "an objective criterion of moral accountability." Thus, John Paul II spoke of an ironic paradox. On one hand, the "effort to establish an international court of justice for crimes against humanity is an expression of the demand for such a criterion in international public opinion. Yet, ironically, the call for an objective criterion of moral accountability is, in many cases, accompanied by the spread of a relativistic approach to truth, which effectively denies any objective criterion of good and evil." John Paul II believes that the "root of this dilemma, with its serious consequences for the life of society, is the tendency to exalt individual autonomy at the expense of the bonds that unite us and make us responsible for one another. Society needs a coherent vision that embraces both the dignity and inalienable rights of each individual, especially the weakest and most vulnerable, and a clear consciousness of the fundamental values and relationships that ultimately constitute the common good."[7] To this, John Rawls and Maritain would both agree. But with the justification of such, Rawls would likely abandon the company of John Paul II, who

6. ZENIT, May 26, 2000.
7. Ibid.

goes on to speak of "a humanism that flows from the truth of the human person, created in the image of God and, therefore, possessing an inviolable dignity and inalienable rights, including the fundamental right to religious freedom." John Paul II continues, "From this vision of the human person there rises that true and noble concept of human society, which recognizes that we are responsible for one another, and which, therefore, demands an ethic of solidarity. This is why it becomes especially urgent to construct an ever more deeply rooted ethic of solidarity and culture of dialogue, since these alone are the path of a peaceful future."[8]

Both Rawls and Maritain recognize that world government subject to what Rawls calls "the law of peoples" is utopian. Maritain wrote at the time that Robert M. Hutchins, Mortimer Adler, and Stringfellow Barr were absorbed in the Chicago discussions on world government. Maritain himself took part in the drafting of the United Nations Universal Declaration of Human Rights in 1948. The European Union was yet to come; so, too, the United Nations Tribunal on War Crimes. Maritain and his Chicago colleagues were right in foreseeing their necessity. In spite of this and other international cooperation on many fronts, world government remains as utopian as ever. Within the European Union itself, where a shared cultural heritage might be expected to promote unity, present conflict suggests almost insurmountable difficulties. How much more difficult would it be to unite Islamic, Chinese, Hindu, and Buddhist cultures. On a purely theoretical level one may discern a common quest for human fulfillment, but the cultural and political barriers are deep and undermine the basic insights that should promote cooperation if not unity. Solidarity is elusive. Maritain in the work under discussion recognized as much.

The United Nations, he was convinced, can only reflect the poli-

8. Ibid.

cies of the sovereign states whose decisions it merely implements. Maritain speaks of the need to sweep away the obstacles caused by the myth of states as sovereign persons. Christopher Morris, in his study of the modern state, acknowledges Maritain's assessment in a footnote, "For a Catholic argument against sovereignty, see Jacques Maritain, *Man and the State.*"[9] Like Maritain, Morris criticizes Hobbes and Rousseau as he builds his case against sovereignty. Morris is convinced that the notion of sovereignty is of little use in understanding the nature and jurisdiction of modern states.[10] "[I] believe," he writes, "that our discussion of 'international' questions might be helped by abandoning it. Instead of talking about sovereignty, we might examine the sorts of independence that states and peoples currently possess and determine which kinds are worth preserving and strengthening, and which should be weakened."[11]

The modern state, he observes, has grown inevitably stronger in supervising national life. Its external relations and foreign policy are relations between supreme entities in their harsh mutual competition. Returning to Maritain, he believes that two main obstacles prevent the establishment of lasting peace: 1) the absolute sovereignty of modern states, and 2) the fact that no world political organization corresponds to the material unification which is the result of economic interdependence.[12] It must be realized that nations are no longer autonomous in their economic life; they are even only half autonomous in their political life because their political life is impaired by the lasting threat of war and, Maritain adds, also by the interference in domestic affairs by the ideology and pressure of other nations. Modern bodies politic have ceased in actual fact to be sovereign; they are no longer fully autonomous.

9. Morris, *An Essay,* 47.
10. Ibid., 226.
11. Ibid., 226–27.
12. Maritain, *Man and the State,* 194.

Particular nations or states are no longer perfect societies in the Thomistic sense. Only an international community politically organized can claim to be the perfect society. By virtue of natural law and *jus gentium* or the common law of civilization, nations and states can fulfill their obligation to the community of the whole world.[13]

Particular bodies politic, our so-called nation states, have grown incapable of achieving self-sufficiency and ensuring peace. It is the international society, not the particular state, which fulfills the traditional definition of perfect society, that is, a self-sufficient body.

Once particular bodies politic have become parts of a politically organized whole, they will have to fulfill their obligations to the whole, not only by natural law and *jus gentium* but also by virtue of positive laws which the politically organized world society will establish. Such a world state will require legislative, executive, and judicial power with the coercive power necessary to enforce the law. Wary of a "dangerous utopia," Maritain says of himself that as an Aristotelian he is not much of an idealist, yet he holds the world society proposed in Hutchins's *A Preliminary Draft for a World Constitution* to be "a great idea, a sound and right idea."[14]

But is world government possible? If the basic political reality is, as Maritain insists, the body politic, not the state, can there be a passage from the present state of affairs to world government? A state without a body politic or a political society of its own is "a world brain without a world body," a veritable super-state superimposed on and interfering with the life of particular states. It is not through the delegation of the various governments, Maritain says, it is through the free suffrage of men and women that the world state is to be founded and maintained. If a world political

13. Ibid., 198.
14. Ibid., 201.

society is some day founded, it will be the result of an uncoerced common will to live together, something freely chosen, not imposed by force, or out of fear of danger. "Fear of war is not and never has been the reason for which men have wanted to form a political society."[15]

When men acquire the will to live together in a worldwide society, it will be because they will to have a will to achieve a worldwide common task. What task indeed? "The most significant synonym of living together is suffering together," writes Maritain. "The very existence of a world-wide society," writes Maritain, "will also imply a certain—relative no doubt, yet quite serious and appreciable—equalization of the standards of life of all individuals." People of the occidental nations would have to accept a lowering of their standards of life.[16] This would require a kind of moral heroism for which they are badly prepared. It will be necessary for them to assume new obligations and sacrifices. But this is the price of peace. The criterion of material success would have to yield to the criterion of the common good.

One body politic is one organized people. But the unity of a world body politic cannot be the unity which characterizes nations. "It would be not even a federal unity, but rather . . . a pluralist unity, taking place only through the lasting diversity of the particular bodies politic, and fostering that diversity."[17] A society of free men implies common tenets which are at the core of its very existence. "A genuine democracy implies a fundamental agreement between minds and wills on the basis of life in common." It must be aware of itself and its principles, and it must be capable of defending and promoting them.

The intellectual commitment which democracy requires is not a religious one but a civic or secular faith, a common human out-

---

15. Ibid., 207.   16. Ibid., 208.
17. Ibid., 209.

look. "A genuine democracy cannot impose on its citizens or demand from them as a condition of their belonging to the city any philosophic or any religious creed."[18]

To those who suggest that the independence of nations would be jeopardized by a world society, Maritain responds that independence is better assured by the creation of a world political society than by its absence. "The States would have to surrender their privilege of being sovereign persons, that is, a privilege which they have never possessed."[19] They would have to give up their full independence, something they have already lost. "Yet in their mutual interdependence the nations could achieve a degree of real, though imperfect, independence higher than that they possess now, from the very fact that their inner political life, being freed from the threat of war and from the interference of rival nations, could become more autonomous in actual fact than it is at present."[20]

Rawls says much the same. The global society which he envisages will be that of a group of satisfied peoples. "In view of their fundamental interests being satisfied, they will have no reason to go to war with one another. The familiar motives for war would be absent: such peoples do not seek to convert others to their religions, nor to conquer greater territory, nor to wield political power over another people."[21]

At the time that Maritain wrote, McGeorge Bundy disagreed. A world state, Bundy thought, would result in the extension of bureaucratic power from a central office to all aspects of national life. McGeorge Bundy had a point. Europeans today complain of Brussels and a bloated bureaucracy which determines aspects of life even in rural France and Spain.

The commonness of international travel and global television

---

18. Ibid., 210.   19. Ibid., 211.
20. Ibid.   21. Rawls, *Law of Peoples,* 19.

has driven home for all to see the diversity of the world's peoples, their beliefs, cultures, and living standards. Western respect for the rule of law, the sanctity of human life, and the rights of private property, although eroding even in the West, is not shared universally. Utopian hopes of a global unity of outlook, even in the minimal sense identified by Rawls, are not likely to be forthcoming in the foreseeable future. Should we be driven to despair? Only if we are hopelessly utopian.

This brief comparison of Rawls and Maritain, separated by fifty years, has clearly shown that men of different intellectual traditions can recognize common social, indeed global, needs and achieve a *modus vivendi* in an attempt to meet those needs. In the work-a-day world of global politics, the two are not far apart. Western culture, admitted or not, provides the backdrop, but in spite of economic interdependence and the commercial success of Western media and the marketing of Western products, is a world culture possible?

Maritain at one point says that sooner or later "states will be obliged to make a choice for or against the Gospel."[22] That may be true. The prospects either way are awesome. Short of the unity which only Christ can provide, the concept of a world government based on a universal subscription to the law of peoples may serve a useful heuristic role. Perhaps it has already done so. We have come a long way since the founding of the United Nations at San Francisco a mere half-century ago.

22. Maritain, *Man and the State*, 159.

VIII

MARITAIN ON
THE CHURCH OF CHRIST

Maritain's last complete book, *De l'Église du Christ,* was published in English translation in the year of his death.[1] It was ignored by the secular media and given scant notice in the Catholic
press. It followed by seven years the publication of *Paysan de la
Garonne* (1966),[2] which had earned Maritain the enmity of the
Catholic left for its critique of some of the theology developing in
the wake of Vatican II. John Courtney Murray in *We Hold These
Truths* (1960) noted happily that the Church in North America was
not divided between left and right as it was with destructive consequences in Europe. By the close of Vatican II, the European virus
had spread to North America. Maritain, who had been the darling
of the liberal Catholic intelligentsia because of his social philosophy, was suddenly ostracized, his later works ignored. For Maritain
a liberal social policy did not presuppose a liberal Catholic theology, certainly not one at war with the intellectual heritage of the
Church.

1. Jacques Maritain, *De l'Église du Christ: la personne de l'Église et son personnel,*
trans. Joseph W. Evans *On the Church of Christ: The Person of the Church and Her Personnel* (Notre Dame: University of Notre Dame Press, 1973).
2. Jacques Maritain, *Le Paysan de la Garonne,* trans. M. Cuddihy and E. Hughes, *The
Peasant of the Garonne* (New York: Holt, Rinehart, and Winston, 1968).

In none of his critical studies does Maritain present himself as a theologian. He is a Catholic layman, a philosopher of rank, noticing the ambiguities, inconsistencies and repudiations of key elements of the Catholic faith by prominent and regrettably influential theologians, who still called themselves somewhat dubiously "Catholic." No stranger to debate, Maritain challenged deviant positions with his customary acuity but without much success. No surprise there: the left characteristically avoids debate, preferring to ignore or ridicule its critics, which it easily does with the aid of a willing secular media. In the case of Maritain, he was simply ignored although one can find snide comments in the writings of a number of Catholic authors.

Maritain's ill treatment aside, his work proved to be prescient in a number of ways. Two recent Vatican documents, *Fides et Ratio* and *Dominus Iesus,* carry elements of the debate, emphasizing the importance of philosophy to theology and the tendency of the ecumenical dialogue to blur irreconcilable differences in the interest of accommodation.

In *De l'Église du Christ* Maritain speaks of the "profoundly troubled historical moment" at which he was writing. He calls himself "an old Christian philosopher who has thought about the mystery of the Church for sixty years."[3] He is appalled by the appreciable number of pseudo-theologians who employ themselves to destroy the treasure of truth which is the Church's responsibility to transmit. His work, he says, should not be read as a work of apologetics. It presupposes the Catholic faith and is addressed primarily to those who share that faith.

Speaking of ecumenism, he decries the search for a spurious universalism, the first condition of which seems to be indifference with respect to truth. It is foolish, he holds, to attempt to unite all Christians in spite of their dissidences and all men in spite of the

3. Maritain, *De l'Église,* v.

diversity of their beliefs. The great utopian ideal—unity of all Christians—can only be achieved with a complete disregard for the truth. One hears of "ecumenical dialogue" but not "ecumenical friendship." Is it not friendship, he asks, which is first required; well-established habits of friendship, created by fraternal banquets, eating, drinking and smoking together, conversing at random and joking? Such is far more useful than "the meetings of commissions with their definite programs, their reports, and their speeches."[4] "The meal taken in common is a natural rite of human friendship."

Four decades subsequent to the close of the Second Vatican Council it is apparent that something unintended occurred. The Church entered the Council in a self-confident, if not triumphant, mood. At the opening of the twenty-first century, the Church remains shaken by the sparseness of vocations to the priesthood and to the religious life and, except for some encouraging pockets in Europe and North America, by the fall in Mass attendance, and neglect of the sacrament of penance. It is commonly acknowledged that the Church has ceased to be a significant cultural factor in its former strongholds. The vague and ambiguous documents issued by the Council, in spite of its attempt in the words of *Gaudium et Spes* to read "the signs of the time . . . interpreting them in the light of the Gospel," lent themselves to misinterpretation. The clear, crisp teaching of a catechetical Church was lost to ecumenical accommodation, noble sentiment, and hollow-sounding abstractions and platitudes. Among the faithful it was thought disloyal to question or to criticize the fruit of the Council and its documents, this at the same time that deviant theologians were invoking them in support of dubious assertions. Maritain, the old philosopher, was free from sanctions and spoke his mind. Today

4. Ibid., 111.

with the unraveling of Catholic institutions worldwide he may be regarded as prescient, although his view was shared by many whose piety led them to remain silent.

With the average Catholic layman, Maritain would have done with "the tempest of wildly diffused foolish ideas" that have caused sorrow and confusion among the faithful. He would "have done with the demythization of doctrine and the secularization or profanization of a Christianity which our new doctors and spiritual guides would like to entrust into the hands of the sociologist, of the psychoanalysts, of the structuralists, of the Marcusists, of the phenomenologists, and of the pioneers of technocracy."[5]

The subtitle of *On the Church of Christ* is indicative of a distinction that is crucial to an understanding of the Church; "Churchmen will never be the Church," in Maritain's judgment. One can take a detached view, making positive and negative assessments of the activity of Churchmen throughout the centuries while remaining confident of the holiness of the Church itself.

His fundamental distinction runs through the work, that is, the difference between the "person of the Church" and "her personnel," that is, between the Church visible to the intellect and the Church as visible to the eyes. "The person of the Church," writes Maritain, "can be holy while being composed of members who are all sinners to some degree."[6] Indeed, members who are holy can be guilty of gross error in their prudential judgments. Noble purposes can be pursued by ignoble means or frustrated by actions gone awry or by miscalculation and adverse circumstances.

That distinction made, Maritain defends the person of the Church while admitting the evils perpetrated in her name by the Crusades, the Inquisition, the suppression of the Albigensians, the

5. Ibid., 241.
6. Ibid., 138.

imprisonment of Galileo, the execution of Joan, and the burning
of Savonarola and Giordano Bruno. No critic or cynic is likely to
draw a longer list of the "sins of the Church," for the most part
grievous errors of judgment by otherwise noble-minded "Churchmen."

It is against this backdrop of acknowledged failure that Maritain assesses from a layman's point of view the successes and failures of the Second Vatican Council. But his chronicle of admitted
failures is only one aspect of an inquiry, an inquiry that is essentially a hymn of praise by a man clearly in love with his church. A
short section paying tribute to Our Lady is equal to that of any
poet for its beauty and depth.

In his defense of the Church, Maritain can be harsh in his in-
dictment of her personnel. Clearly the episodes he addresses are a
bit more complex than he makes them out to be. To focus only
on the Galileo affair, a scholar writing from a purely secular perspective, Giorgio Diaz de Santillana, defends the Church against
charges of gross mistreatment of Galileo, largely because the heliocentric theory advanced by Galileo was not demonstrated until the
early nineteenth century.[7] Bellarmine's Aristotelian view of scientific explanation was pertinent to the demand that Galileo defend
his view as a theoretical explanation of observed phenomena and
not as an established fact. De Santillana's respect for the social context in which the sometimes unpleasant Galileo was often out of
bounds with his incursions into biblical theology places the whole
episode in a more humane light and is less condemnatory of the
actions of the churchmen than Maritain would allow. William A.
Wallace's study of Galileo corroborates de Santillana's judgment
that Galileo may have brought most of his troubles upon himself

7. Giorgio Diaz de Santillana, *Crime of Galileo* (Chicago: University of Chicago
Press, 1955).

by his intemperate behavior toward authorities who may have censured him for reasons other than his heliocentric theory, which theretofore did not disturb ecclesiastical authority as long as it was advanced as a theory.

There is one area where Maritain forcefully comes to the defense of the Churchmen—namely, the treatment of the Jews. "The hatred of the Jewish people in the Middle Ages was the deed of the populace and of many in the bourgeoisie and in the nobility and many in the lower clergy. The high personnel of the Church, the Papacy above all, remained free from it."[8] He continues, "The Popes, even the ones most severe in their legislation, never knew this hatred."[9] It was in the papal states that the Jews fared best. "During the whole of the Middle Ages and the darkest periods of the latter, it was the Popes who were their greatest protectors and defenders."[10]

Maritain points out that the Bull of Calixtus II (1120) condemning the violences against the Jews and their baptism under constraint was confirmed at least twenty-two times up to the middle of the eighteenth century. "The episcopal body as a whole kept itself free from religious hatred of the Jewish people."[11] By contrast, hatred of the Jews was intense in Luther and in Voltaire. Although religious anti-Semitism may have disappeared long before Maritain's day, he praises Vatican II for completely eradicating the idea of the Jewish people as the "deicide-people," the religious anti-Semitism which long soiled Christendom. The Council insists upon the friendship to be developed and consolidated between Jews and Christians. "It seems to me," writes Maritain, "that in order to authenticate the friendship in question prerequires of the two sides a purification of thought: it is necessary that the Chris-

---

8. Maritain, *De l'Église,* 167.   9. Ibid.
10. Ibid., 168.   11. Ibid.

tian understand truly that God has not rejected, but has always continued to love the children of Israel, and that it is *His love* which has permitted this long passion and it will be necessary for the Jews to understand truly that it is not the will for power, but the *charity of Christ,* which animates the effort of the Church toward men."[12] Maritain is not naive. He recognizes that dislike for the Jews, quite apart from religious motivation, is often based on behavioral or ethnic considerations.

Some are inclined to rejoice that finally the church recognizes that she errs, that finally she confesses her fallibility, that finally one can proclaim that she has not ceased to accumulate mistakes in the diverse epochs of her history. This is the view of numerous theologians "who erect themselves into a magisterium—a 'scientific' magisterium—with which the sole true magisterium would be doubled."[13] They seem to be dangerously embarked on a concerted effort to undermine Roman authority.

Inexactness of language often leads some to attribute to the Church an act or decision of her directing personnel without distinguishing whether the latter has acted as "proper cause" or as an "instrument of the Church herself." Maritain reminds his readers that it is only the solemn magisterium of the Pope speaking alone (and not through a Roman Congregation), or when he speaks "conjointly with the bishops assembled in General Council" (solemn magisterium) or "conjointly with the bishops dispersed throughout the world" (ordinary magisterium) that it is the person of the Church herself speaking and acting, the Church one, holy, and infallible. "The person of the Church is there, before our eyes, manifestly at work, through the magisterium when it teaches infallibly. She is there—and in what a sublime manner!—through the Sacrifice of the Mass . . . the Sacraments, through each Bap-

12. Ibid., 174.
13. Ibid., 234.

tism, each absolution received, each Communion in the Body and Blood of Christ."[14]

"Finally even when one of the members of her personnel uses badly his juridical authority or his moral authority, the person of the Church is still there in a certain indirect manner, which does not render her responsible for that which he does in betraying her spirit."[15]

Maritain recognizes that writing in "the midst of a tempest of widely diffused foolish ideas,"[16] much of what he says will displease many. Yet he hopes that however poorly he has said it, that in fifty years time the judgment may be made that "after all, it was not so stupid." In fact, Maritain could be read as a preamble to the declaration, *Dominus Iesus,*[17] which seeks to call to mind certain indispensable elements of Christian doctrine by providing a clear description of the nature of the Church and her mission. The document proclaims, "God has willed that the Church founded by Him be the instrument for the salvation of *all* humanity. . . . This truth does not lessen the sincere respect which the Church has for the religions of the world."[18] Yet the fullness of Christianity is to be found only within the Church, in Christ Himself who is "the way, the truth, and the life."

Interreligious dialogue is part of the Church's evangelizing mission, but "equality, which is the presumption of interreligious dialogue, refers to equal personal dignity of the parties in the dialogue, not to doctrinal content, nor even less to the position of Jesus Christ—who is God himself made man—in relation to the founders of other religions."[19]

---

14. Ibid., 239.   15. Ibid.

16. Ibid., 241.

17. Promulgated June 16, 2000, with the approval of John Paul II and signed by Joseph Cardinal Ratzinger, Prefect of the Congregation for the Doctrine of the Faith.

18. Ibid., 14.   19. Ibid., 14–15.

One has only to study the texts of the reformers to discern how incompatible are the doctrines advanced by Luther and Calvin, for example, with those of the Catholic Church. On the issue of the relation of faith and reason addressed by John Paul II in his 1998 encyclical, *Fides et Ratio,* Luther stands in the tradition of Tatian and Tertullian, both of whom died outside of the Church, not in that of Justin Martyr, Athenagoras and Clement of Alexandria. Contradictory positions cannot be held simultaneously, in spite of good will. Maritain found it necessary to repeat this truism in both *De l'Église* and the earlier *Paysan.* John Paul II's encouragement of extended philosophical training in the seminaries may, if implemented, mitigate the romantic blurring of truth in the interest of a spurious intellectual ecumenism which Maritain feared.

In discussing Maritain's view of the Church, one is drawn to the work of Vladimir Soloviev,[20] 1853–1900, a philosopher and layman who, like Maritain, was concerned about the Church, but in his case from the vantage point of Orthodox Christianity. It may not be inaccurate to present Soloviev as a near contemporary of Maritain since his work was suppressed in his lifetime and largely eclipsed by decades of Soviet domination. Like Maritain he wrote about the Church he loved—in Maritain's language, the "person of the Church." His witness to Christianity was praised by John Paul II in an address at Castel Gondolfo.[21] Leo XIII had called him the "sage from the East." Hans Urs von Balthasar praised him for providing "beyond question the most profound vindication and the most comprehensive philosophical statement of the Christian totality in modern times."[22]

20. Sometimes his surname is rendered as Sergveyevich or Solovyou.

21. ZENIT, July 30, 2000.

22. Untranslated Collected Works of Vladimir Soloviev (SSVS), vol. 13,188, as quoted by Gregory Flazov, "Vladimir Solovyov and the Idea of Papacy," *Communio,* 24, Spring 1997: 130.

Both Maritain and Soloviev grounded their thoughts about the Church in patristic Christianity. For Maritain the Great Schism was the work of men, the Church's personnel. With Maritain, Soloviev affirms that Christianity is the agent empowered by Christ to bring humanity into the Kingdom of God, not only at the personal level but also at the social and political.

Toward the end of his life the goal of a united Christendom became Soloviev's primary concern. Convinced that Catholic and Orthodox Churches were fundamentally one, as evidenced by basic agreements along doctrinal, sacramental, and hierarchically apostolic lines, he sought to advance their unity "sundered *de facto* and not *de jure*." He found Orthodox Christianity susceptible to excessive determination by nationalist and statist attitudes, but he was equally critical, not unlike Maritain, of the papacy in its historical tendency to use its ecclesial authority to pursue worldly ends.

While Maritain makes an important distinction between the Church and her personnel, Soloviev advances a similar distinction between the Church of Rome and the Latin Church, that is, between the functions of the Pope as Bishop of Rome and as Patriarch of the West. "It is the Church of Rome, not the Latin Church, that is the *mater et magistra omnium Ecclesiarum:* it is the Bishop of Rome, and not the Western Patriarch, who speaks infallibly *ex cathedra*." And Soloviev adds, "We ought not to forget that there was a time when the Bishops of Rome were Greeks."[23] One could find many parallels between the thought of Maritain and Soloviev, especially on the role of religion in society, in law and morality, and in the treatment of the Jews.[24]

Two laymen, philosophers, united by the Catholic faith and a

23. Ibid., 131.

24. Cf. *Politics, Law, Morality: Essays by V. S. Soloviev,* ed. and trans. Vladimir Wozniuk (New Haven: Yale University Press, 2000).

common love for classical philosophy, especially Aristotle, writing across the divide wrought by the Great Schism, contribute by virtue of their professional skills to a common understanding of the Church, later taught magisterially in *Fides et Ratio* and *Dominus Iesus.*

BIBLIOGRAPHY

Aristotle. *De Anima*. In *Basic Works of Aristotle*. Edited by Richard McKeon. New York: Random House, 1941.

Bergson, Henri. *The Two Sources of Religion and Morality*. New York: Holt, 1935.

Butchvarov, P. *Resemblance and Identity*. Bloomington, Ind.: Indiana University Press, 1966.

Cicero, Marcus Tullius. *De Legibus*. Loeb Classical Library, Book II. Cambridge: Harvard University Press, 1966.

Dawson, Christopher. *Religion and the Rise of Western Culture*. New York: Sheed and Ward, 1950.

de Santillana, Giorgio Diaz. *Crime of Galiteo*. Chicago: University of Chicago Press, 1955.

Devlin, Patrick. *The Enforcement of Morals*. London: Oxford University Press, 1965.

Dewey, John. *Experience and Nature*. New York: Macmillan, 1948.

———. *Art as Experience*. New York: Minton Balch, 1934.

———. *A Common Faith*. New Haven: Yale University Press, 1934.

Dougherty, Jude P. "Dewey and the Value of Religion." *New Scholasticism* 51 (1977): 303–27.

Durkheim, Emile. *The Elementary Forms of Religious Life*. Translated by J. W. Swain. New York: Collier, 1961.

D'Entrèves, Alexander P. *The Notion of the State*. Oxford: Clarendon Press, 1967.

Gallagher, D., and I. Gallagher. *The Achievement of Jacques and Raïssa Maritain*. Garden City, N.Y.: Doubleday, 1962.

Gracia, Jorge J. E. *Introduction to the Problem of Individuation in the Middle Ages*. Washington, D.C.: The Catholic University of America Press, 1984.

———. *Individuality: An Essay on the Foundations of Metaphysics*. Albany: State University of New York Press, 1988.

———, editor. *Individuation and Identity in Early Modern Philosophy*. Albany: State University of New York Press, 1994.

———, editor. *Individuation in Scholasticism: The Later Middle Ages and the Counter-Reformation (1150–1650)*. Albany: State University of New York Press, 1994.

Harré, Rom. *Principles of Scientific Explanation*. Chicago: University of Chicago Press, 1970.

Hart, Charles A. *Thomistic Metaphysics*. Englewood Cliffs, N.J.: Prentice Hall, 1959.

Howard, A. E. Dick. "Up Against the Wall: The Uneasy Separation of Church and State."

In *Church, State, and Politics,* edited by Jaye B. Hensel. Washington, D.C.: The Roscoe Pound American Trial Lawyers Foundation, 1982.

Hutchinson, William T. and William M. E. Rachals, editors. *Papers of James Madison.* Chicago: University of Chicago Press, 1962.

Kant, Immanuel. *Knitik der neinen Veruunt.* Translated by Norman Kemp Smith as *Critique of Pure Reason.* New York: St. Martin's Press, 1965.

King, N. Q. *The Emperor Theodosius and the Establishment.* Philadelphia: Westminster Press, 1960.

Kuklick, Bruce. *Josiah Royce: An Intellectual Biography.* New York: Bobbs-Merrill, 1972.

Maritain, Jacques. *Art et scolastique.* Translated by J. F. Scanlan as *Art and Scholasticism.* New York: Sheed and Ward, 1930.

————. *Art and Scholasticism.* New York: Scribners, 1960.

————. *Christianity and Democracy.* London: Geoffrey Bles, 1945.

————. *Court traité de l'existence et de l'existant.* Translated by L. Galantière and G. B. Phelan as *Existence and the Existent.* New York: Pantheon, 1948.

————. *Creative Intuition in Art and Poetry* (The A. W. Mellon Lectures). New York: Pantheon, 1953.

————. *Degrés du savoir.* Translated by G. B. Phelan from the fourth French edition as *The Degrees of Knowledge.* New York: Scribner's, 1959.

————. *Distinguer pour unir ou les degrés du savior.* Translated by B. Wall and M. Adamson as *The Degrees of Knowledge.* London: Geoffrey Bles, The Century Press, 1937.

————. *Le docteur angelique.* Translated by J. F. Scanlan as *St. Thomas Aquinas: Angel of the Schools* (London: Sheed and Ward, 1931). Paris: Desclée, 1930.

————. *De l'Église du Christ.* Translated by J. W. Evans as *On the Church of Christ: the Person of the Church and Her Personnel.* Notre Dame, Ind.: University of Notre Dame Press, 1973.

————. *Eléménts de philosophie.* Translated by E. I. Watkin as *Elements of Philosophy.* New York: Sheed and Ward, 1930.

————. *Humanisme intégral.* Translated as *True Humanism.* New York: Charles Scribner's, 1938.

————. *Introduction générale à la philosophie.* Paris: Pierre Téqui, 1921. Translated from the 11th French and edited by E. I. Watkin as *Introduction to Philosophy.* New York: Sheed and Ward, 1937.

————. *Man and the State.* Chicago: University of Chicago Press, 1951.

————. *Paysan de la Garonne.* Translated by M. Cuddihy and E. Hughes as *The Peasant of the Garonne.* New York: Holt, Rinehart and Winston, 1968.

————. *La personne et le bien commun.* Translated by J. J. Fitzgerald as *Person and the Common Good.* London: Geoffrey Bles, 1948.

————. *La Philosophie morale, examen historique et critiques des grand.* Translated by Marshall Suther et al. as *Moral Philosophy: An Historical and Critical Survey of the Great Systems.* New York: Scribner's, 1964.

————. *La Philosophie de la nature.* Paris: Pierre Téqui, 1935. Translated by Imelda C. Byrne as *Philosophy of Nature.* New York: Philosophical Library, 1951.

———. *The Range of Reason.* New York: Charles Scribner's, 1952.

———. *Redeeming the Time.* London: Geoffrey Bles, 1943.

———. *Reflections on America.* New York: Charles Scribner's, 1958.

———. *Responsibility of the Artist.* New York: Scribner's, 1960.

———. *St. Thomas Aquinas: Angel of the Schools.* Translated by J. F. Scanlan from the original French, *Le docteur angelique* (Paris: Desclée, 1930). London: Sheed and Ward, 1931.

———. *Science et sagesse.* Paris: Labergerie, 1935. Translated by B. Wall as *Science and Wisdom.* New York: Charles Scribner's Sons, 1940.

———. *Sept leçons sur l'être et les premieres principes de la raison spéculative.* Translated by B. Wall as *A Preface to Metaphysics: Seven Lectures on Being.* New York: Sheed and Ward, 1948.

———. *Theonas.* Translated by F. J. Sheed. New York: Sheed and Ward, 1933.

Matthews, John. *Western Aristocracies and the Imperial Court.* Oxford: Clarendon Press, 1975.

Mauer, Armand. *Introduction to Thomas Aquinas. The Division and Methods of the Sciences.* Toronto: Pontifical Institute of Medieval Studies, 1963.

Mayer, Milton. *Robert Maynard Hutchins: A Memoir.* Berkeley: University of California Press, 1993.

Meiland, J. W. *Talking about Particulars.* New York: Humanities Press, 1970.

Mill, John Stuart. *Nature and Utility of Religion.* New York: The Liberal Arts Press, 1958.

———. "Plan of the Scientific Operations Necessary for Reorganizing Society." In *On Intellectuals,* edited by Philip Rieff. Garden City, N.Y.: Doubleday, 1969.

Morino, Claudio. *Church and State in the Teaching of St. Ambrose.* Translated by M. Joseph Costelloe. Washington, D.C.: The Catholic University of America Press, 1969.

Morris, Christopher. *An Essay on the Modern State.* Cambridge: Cambridge University Press, 1998.

Murray, John Courtney. *We Hold These Truths.* New York: Sheed and Ward, 1960.

Nesbit, Robert. *Twilight of Authority.* New York: Oxford University Press, 1979.

Ortega y Gasset, José. *The Dehumanization of Art.* Princeton, N.J.: Princeton University Press, 1968.

Owens, Joseph. "Judgment and Truth in Aquinas." *Medieval Studies* 32 (1970): 138–58.

———. "Thomas Aquinas." In *Individuation in Scholasticism and the Later Middle Ages,* edited by Jorge J. E. Gracia. Albany: State University of New York Press, 1994.

Paredi, Angelo. *St. Ambrose: His Life and Times.* Notre Dame, Ind.: University of Notre Dame Press, 1964.

Rawls, John. *Law of Peoples.* Cambridge: Harvard University Press, 1999.

Royce, Josiah. *Fugitive Essays.* Cambridge: Harvard University Press, 1925.

Rutland, Robert A., editor. *The Papers of George Mason 1725–1791.* Chapel Hill, N.C.: University of North Carolina Press, 1970.

Shook, Laurence K. *Etienne Gilson.* Toronto: Pontifical Institute of Mediaeval Studies, 1984.

Soloviev, V. S. *Politics, Law, Morality: Essays by V. S. Soloviev.* Edited and translated by Vladimir Wozniuk. New Haven: Yale University Press, 2000.

Strawson, P. F. *Individuals: An Essay in Descriptive Metaphysics.* London: Methuen, 1959.

Thomas Aquinas. *Summa Theologiae.* Translated by the Fathers of the English Dominican Province, 3 vols. New York: Benzinger Brothers, 1947.

Tolstoy, Leo N. *What Is Art?* Translated from the Russian original by A. Maude. New York: Bobbs Merrill, 1960.

Voltaire. *Notebooks.* Edited by Theodore Testerman. 2 vols. Geneva: Institut et Musée, 1952.

von Simson, Otto. "Suger of St. Denis." In *The Gothic Cathedral.* New York: Pantheon, 1962.

Wallace, William A. *The Modeling of Nature: Philosophy of Science and Philosophy of Nature in Synthesis.* Washington, D.C.: The Catholic University of America Press, 1996.

INDEX

Jacques Maritain: An Intellectual Profile was designed and composed in Minion with
   Hiroshige display type by Kachergis Book Design of Pittsboro, North Carolina.
   It was printed on sixty-pound Glatfelter Writers Offset Smooth and bound
        by Edwards Brothers, Inc., Lillington, North Carolina.